1983

MEXICO TODAY

MEXICO
TODAY

Edited by

Tommie Sue Montgomery

A Publication of the
Institute for the Study of Human Issues
Philadelphia

Manufactured in the United States of America

1 2 3 4 5 6 7 8 9 10 11 12 13 89 88 87 86 85 84 83 82

Library of Congress Cataloging in Publication Data

Main entry under title:

Mexico today.

    1. Mexico—Addresses, essays, lectures.   2. Mexico—Foreign
relations—1946-   —Addresses, essays, lectures.   I. Montgomery,
Tommie Sue.
F1208.M623   972.08'3   81-20152
ISBN 0-89727-030-4   AACR2
ISBN 0-89727-040-1 (pbk.)

For information, write:

Director of Publications
ISHI
3401 Science Center
Philadelphia, Pennsylvania 19104
U.S.A.

A Public Affairs Publication of the

Center for Inter-American Relations

The Center for Inter-American Relations has worked, since it began operations in 1967, to build in the United States an understanding of the other nations in the Western hemisphere. Through its Literature, Visual, and Performing Arts programs, the Center promotes a broader awareness in the U.S. of the cultural achievements of the Americas. In numerous meetings scheduled each year by the Center's Public Affairs program, political, social, and economic subjects of inter-American interest are discussed and debated. The Center offers an unofficial platform from which public and private leaders, scholars, and social critics can make their thoughts known to diverse international audiences.

The purpose of this publication is to expand the Center's efforts by reaching those interested in inter-American affairs who are not able to participate personally in the Center's activities. We hope that this work, along with previous and forthcoming volumes sponsored by the Public Affairs program, will contribute significantly to the permanent body of research and commentary.

Ronald G. Hellman

Contents

PART 3   MEXICO AND THE WORLD

Acknowledgments

This book and the symposium from which it is drawn would not have been possible without the hard work and support of many individuals and institutions. The Mexico Today Symposium was sponsored by the Smithsonian Resident Associate Program, Janet Solinger, Director; the Center for Inter-American Relations, Roger Stone, President; and Meridian House International, Joseph John Jova, President. Thanks also to the many businesses and foundations, both in the United States and Mexico, whose support made the symposium possible. In particular the generous assistance of the National Endowment for the Humanities and the National Endowment for the Arts was instrumental in making this multifaceted celebration a reality.

As for this volume, I would like to thank first the National Endowment for the Humanities, whose grant has made its publication possible. Second, a note of appreciation is extended to *Vuelta* and to El Colegio de México for permission to reprint several of the essays. Finally, I wish to thank Ronald Hellman, Public Affairs Director of the Center for Inter-American Relations, whose confidence in my editorial abilities has not, I hope, been misplaced; Marilyn Graham, also of the Center, for her typing skills and her unwavering attention to detail; Marsha Grant, whose editorial comments and almost total recall of various details of Mexican history saved me a trip to a distant library; and my family, who provided a distraction-free haven seventy miles from nowhere in central Florida, thereby enabling me to complete this and other projects during a not so long but very hot summer.

Tommie Sue Montgomery

Editor's Note

In the fall of 1978 the cities of Washington, D.C., New York, Atlanta, San Diego, San Francisco, and Los Angeles were treated to a symposium dedicated to the celebration of a nation: its people, its life, its creativity. The nation was Mexico, and the purpose of this national symposium was to give North Americans an opportunity to become better acquainted with their neighbor to the south. The papers included in this volume represent only one portion of the Mexico Today Symposium. The celebration also included exhibits of *tapetes,* costumes, pottery, modern art, and photographs; seminars on pre-Columbian art, architecture and society, women writers, and Mexican flora; art workshops; plays; dance performances; and concerts.

The essays presented here reflect the major themes of a series of panels held during October and November in Washington and New York to discuss Mexico as a nation and a state—and Mexico's relationship with the world in general and the United States in particular. They serve to remind North Americans, as Octavio Paz notes in his opening essay, that Mexico and the United States represent two dimensions of Western civilization: the Catholic, communal culture of Latin America and the Mediterranean, and the Protestant, individualistic culture of North America and northern Europe.

As Paz points out, knowledge does not necessarily imply understanding. While North Americans have amassed enormous amounts of data and written more than a thousand dissertations (and at least as many books) on Mexico, few in the academic world or in the larger population can lay claim to a true understanding of a neighbor whose historic and cultural roots are different from our own.

The value of this book lies in the fact that it provides a means for some of the best and most creative minds of Mexico to speak to their neighbors to the north. The discussions of the original panels were not intended for a specialized audience and neither is this book. If it finds its way into classrooms as a supplementary text, that will be a bonus, for this volume offers an opportunity to all North Americans to put themselves in their neighbors' shoes. If some readers detect an occasional note of resentment or bitterness—even irritation or frustration—they should consider the possibility that there are valid grounds for those feelings. The Mexican thinkers and scholars gathered here argue their cases well; the least we can do is listen equally well.

While there were originally seven panels, I have tried to bring greater coherence to a wide range of topics by organizing them around three themes: the nation, the state, and the nation-state on the world scene. The volume opens, as did the symposium, with an essay by Octavio Paz, who reflects on these three dimensions and elaborates on the factors that separate the U.S. and Mexico, as well as on those that bind us together.

An important aspect of the Mexican nation is its rich and varied cultural life. As noted above, the symposium attempted, with some success, to share with North Americans the many facets of this culture. Because art was so important to the program, it would be unfortunate to give the impression that 'Mexico Today' consisted only of historical, political, and economic analyses. Even though Part 1 is shorter than the sections that follow and cannot capture the full flavor of the symposium, I hope its essays, which deal with Mexico's culture, will give the reader an awareness of the overall scope of the program. To begin this section, Ignacio Bernal, who more than any other individual is responsible for the magnificent National Museum of Anthropology in Mexico City, discusses the pre-Columbian roots of the Mexican nation. Then Josefina Vásquez addresses the problem faced by Mexico's nineteenth-century leaders when they sought to create a nation from a multitude of cultures.

Finally, Rodolfo Stavenhagen elaborates on the continuing difficulties of nation-building in the twentieth century.

Part 2 focuses on the state. Porfirio Muñoz Ledo and Fernando Pérez Correa examine the promise of Mexico's revolution and constitution. Their essays, as well as that of Rafael Segovia, assess the successes, failures, and adaptive capacity of the resulting political system. Luis Unikel turns our attention to the pervasive problem of rapid population growth and its effect on Mexican cities. Victor Urquidi then closes the section and prepares us for the next by reviewing Mexico's industrial growth and critiquing the profit-centered shortcomings of its domestic and foreign investors.

Part 3 examines several aspects of Mexico as a nation-state, with particular attention to relations between the United States and Mexico. Bernardo Sepúlveda Amor places Mexico's development prospects in the context of international trade and finance, and makes a strong case for the development of a new international economic order. Olga Pellicer de Brody then reviews the key factors that have impeded the development of strong political and economic relations with the Third World, and discusses the conditions that now favor such ties. In contrast, the next three essays focus on Mexican-United States relations. Mario Ojeda Gómez analyzes the structure within which those relations occur and defines the major issues that confront the two countries in the '80s. Jorge Bustamante exposes the major misperceptions on the part of North Americans with regard to the undocumented worker phenomenon. In a similar vein, Samuel del Villar demonstrates that the myopia of U.S. policymakers is having negative effects both in the United States and in Mexico. Finally, Jorge Castañeda brings us full circle. As Octavio Paz began by developing the theme of positions and counterpositions between the U.S. and Mexico, Castañeda closes this collection by reminding North Americans that our (frequently ethnocentric) view of the world needs some adjusting.

In closing, I wish to say a word about usage. Latin Americans consistently use *norteamericano* when referring to citizens of the United States. They resent, justifiably, the appropriation of the term "American" as a description of those born between the

Rio Grande and the Canadian border, reasoning that all citizens of the Western Hemisphere are Americans. I have honored this preference and urge my *paisanos* to consider adopting it. I have also made a conscious effort to "neuterize" pronouns. My feminist friends will, I hope, forgive me for leaving one or two passages intact. In those cases, I concluded that any change would destroy the rhythm of the language and/or change the precise meaning the author intended.

Finally, I wish to mention *Visión del México Contemporaneo* (Mexico City: El Colegio de México, 1979), which includes several of the essays published here and is Mexico's *recuerdo* of the celebration in its honor.

Tommie Sue Montgomery

Preface

Joseph John Jova

Octavio Paz, author of the opening essay, has made the observation that in relations between neighboring countries the unforgivable sin is ignorance and lack of understanding. Such a situation exists on both sides of the border, in Mexico with regard to the United States and in the United States with regard to Mexico.

The main purpose of this collection of essays is to help improve understanding of Mexico in our own country by presenting a comprehensive view of our neighbor to the south. In the symposium from which these papers are drawn, the discussion panels, the art exhibits, the poetry readings, the music and dance, the film series, and the academic courses were all designed to give Mexicans themselves the opportunity to tell the Mexican story in all its richness and dynamism.

The intent of the symposium was to provide a learning experience for our own people: an opportunity for cultural enrichment, a chance for a frank exchange of views, a means of increasing understanding and dispelling the myths and stereotypes that exist about a neighboring country. Mexico is a nation long important to the United States, a powerful force in the hemisphere, and one destined to play an ever more crucial role on the world scene. Of course, understanding does not necessarily imply agreement. Obviously, there will always be differences of opinion between us, as both sides have valid viewpoints, but these essays should help clarify the issues and should promote better comprehension of the factors that underlie each side's position.

José Cecilio del Valle, the first foreign minister of an independent Mexico, and himself an American in the broadest sense, wrote: *El mejor estudio de un americano es America.* ("The best subject for an American to study is America.") He continued more or less as follows: "America during the day, when I write; America in the evening, when I think; America at night, when I dream." With the symposium, and now with these papers, all of us, Americans in the broadest sense, can take a step—one of many steps, I hope—to study, to write, to think, to dream of our greater America.

Octavio Paz, whose essay follows, is a creative and dynamic force in contemporary arts and letters. He is Mexico's most distinguished thinker and writer, one of the major poets writing today in Spanish. He has received the International Poetry Grand Prize and is one of the foremost candidates for the Nobel Prize in literature. He has served as Mexico's Ambassador to India, in other diplomatic posts, and in educational work. He is the recipient of numerous honors in the United States, Europe, and other parts of the world. In addition to his poetry and art criticism, he is one of the world's leading political and social critics. His judgments on both the United States and Mexico have sometimes been severe, but they have always been marked by an even-handed objectivity that has won him the respect of his peers throughout the world. It is therefore most fitting that his essay open this collection.

Mexico and the United States: Positions and Counterpositions*

Octavio Paz

The world around us is made up of incessant, contradictory changes and movements. One of the most persistent tendencies of thought is to try to give a meaning to this continuous agitation; in the realm of natural phenomena we have succeeded in distinguishing at least some regular and recurring patterns, though not a definite direction. The universe is enigmatic rather than incoherent. But there is one recalcitrant zone that resists systematic ordering, and will not obey the prescriptions and predictions of science—humanity itself. Human beings may not be the kings of creation, but they are certainly nature's exception. The irreducible particle, the peculiarity that defies all rules and definitions, the elusive, indeterminate element, is not found in the atoms of contemporary physics but in human beings. Scientists marvel at the unexpected and in some ways capricious behavior of elemental particles, but what are these physical eccentricities compared to the psychological and moral extravagances of a Nero or a St. Francis of Assisi?

The history of societies is no less rich in irregularities and oddities than the biographies of individuals. What is anthropology if not the description of unusual customs and frenzied ritu-

---

*Translated by Rachel Phillips.

als? Societies are as unpredictable as individuals, which is why even the greatest of the sociologists have produced a longer and more impressive list of thwarted prophecies than the astrologers and clairvoyants. I am not trying to damn the social sciences with facile arguments. I am merely reminding us of their limits. Though they do not give us laws and formulas as precise as those of physics and chemistry, they give us something just as precious—an understanding of human collectivities. The social sciences may not constitute knowledge, but they do constitute wisdom. I am thinking especially of history, the beginning and end of social studies. Reading Thucydides, Gibbon, or de Tocqueville does not reveal to us the secret laws of human societies, but it opens our eyes to the reality of human beings and teaches us to see them with piety and irony.

History accumulates incoherences and contradictions with a kind of humor at once involuntary and perverse. When I was in India, witnessing the never-ending quarrels between Hindus and Muslims, more than once I asked myself this question: What accident or misfortune of history caused two religions so obviously irreconcilable as Hinduism and Islam to coexist in the same society? The presence of the purest and most intransigent form of monotheism in the bosom of a civilization that has elaborated the most complex and perfect polytheism seemed to me a verification of the indifference with which history perpetrates its cruel paradoxes. But I could hardly be surprised at the contradictory presence in India of Hinduism and Islam. How could I forget that I myself was (and am) part of a no less singular paradox: that of Mexico and the United States.

Our countries are neighbors, condemned to live alongside each other; they are separated, however, more by very profound social, economic, and psychic differences than by physical and political frontiers. These differences are self-evident, and a superficial glance might reduce them to the well-known opposition between development and underdevelopment, wealth and poverty, power and weakness, domination and dependence. But the really fundamental difference is an invisible one, and in addition it is perhaps insuperable. To prove that it has nothing to do with economics or political power, we have only to imagine a Mexico suddenly turned into a prosperous, mighty country, a superpower like the United States. Far from disappearing, the differences would become more acute and more clear-cut. The reason is obvious: these differences are not only quantitative but qualitative; they pertain to the nature of our respective civilizations. What separates us is the very thing that unites us. We are two distinct versions of Western civilization.

Ever since Mexicans began to be aware of a national identity—in about the middle of the eighteenth century—we have been interested in our neighbors. First there was a mixture of curiosity and disdain; later an admiration and enthusiasm that were soon tinged with fear and envy. The idea the Mexican people have of the United States is contradictory, passionate, and impervious to criticism; actually, it is a mythic image rather than an idea. The same can be said of the vision of our intellectuals and writers. Something similar happens with North Americans, be they writers or politicians, business people or only travelers.

I am not forgetting the existence of a small number of remarkable studies by various North American specialists, especially in the fields of archaeology and ancient and modern Mexican history. Unfortunately, praiseworthy though these studies are, they are no substitute for what we need most: understanding. This is all the more difficult because understanding, which is an art and a science, is also a passion. Without any passionate attraction (sympathy or sometimes antipathy) for the other, the encounter from which the spark of understanding springs does not take place. In this sense, the most penetrating observations have perhaps been those of the novelists and poets who have written on Mexican themes. However, their perceptions have been fragmentary and, as Drewey Wayne Gunn has noted in *American and British Writers in Mexico,* they reveal less of the Mexican reality than they do of the authors' personalities. In general, North Americans have not looked for Mexico in Mexico; they have looked for their obsessions, enthusiasms, phobias, hopes, interests—and these are what they have found. In short, the ideas of North Americans and Mexicans about their neighbors are reactions, emotional outbursts. They are images, not documents, passionate judgments rather than descriptions. The history of our relationship is the history of a mutual and stubborn deceit, usually involuntary, though not always so.

Of course, the differences between Mexico and the United States are not imaginary projections but objective realities. Some are quantitative and can be explained by the social, economic, and historical development of the two countries. Others, the more permanent ones, though also the result of history, are not easily definable or measurable. I have already pointed out that they belong to the realm of civilizations, that fluid zone of imprecise contours in which are fused and confused ideas and beliefs, institutions and technologies, styles and morals, fashions and churches, the material culture and that evasive reality that we rather inaccurately call *le genre de peuples*. The concept of civilization is vague, but the same is true of another expression beloved by anthropologists and sociologists—culture.

In any case, civilization is a term that includes both the given elements of a society—social and political institutions, arts, technology, means of production and distribution, rituals, all that goes under the name of culture—and also the internal and external forces that form and change it. Civilization is an eminently historical concept: a civilization is the result of the interaction, in time and by time, of different, interwoven causes on an already determined culture. The idea of civilization implies that of different cultures and nations united by relationships of affinity and opposition. Culture, an anthropological and sociological term, evokes a rather static vision of a society in isolation from others; civilization, an historical term, denotes a group of cultures in movement and in constant interaction.

The discussion of the differences between culture and civilization is age-old. Some will find the duality I have just outlined illusory; others will say, perhaps rightly, that my distinction is cursory, deficient, or unclear. The last word on this subject has not been heard. Whatever opinion we hold, the fact is that the reality to which we give the name civilization does not permit easy definition. It is each society's vision of the world, but it is also its feeling about time; there are nations that are hurrying toward the future, and others whose eyes are fixed on the past.

Civilization is a society's style, its way of living—and of dying. It embraces the erotic and the culinary arts; dancing and burial; courtesy and curses; work and leisure; rituals and festivals; morals and pleasure; punishments and rewards; dealings with the dead and with the beings who people our dreams; ways of owning property and of spending; attitudes toward women and children, old people and strangers, enemies and allies; public debate and soliloquy; eternity and the present; the here-and-now and the beyond. . . . A civilization is not only a system of values, it is a world of forms and codes of behavior, principles and customs, rules and exceptions. It is a table of commandments and a ritual of transgressions and expiations. It is society's visible side—institutions, monuments, ideas, works, things—but it is especially society's submerged, invisible side—beliefs, desires, fears, repressions, dreams.

The points of the compass have served to orient us in history as well as in space. The East/West duality soon acquired a more symbolic than geographic significance, and became an emblem of the opposition between civilizations. The same happened with North and South. The East/West opposition has always been considered basic and primordial; it alludes to the movement of the sun, and is therefore an image of the direction and meaning of our living and dying. The East/West relationship symbolizes two directions, two attitudes, two civilizations. When they cross, there is the clash of war or, more rarely, that miraculous conjunction that we call "the union of opposites." The North/South duality refers more to the opposition between different ways of life and different sensibilities. The contrasts between North and South can be oppositions within the same civilization.

Clearly, the opposition between Mexico and the United States belongs to the North/South duality, as much from the geographic as the symbolic point of view. It is an ancient opposition that was already unfolding in pre-Columbian America, so that it antedates the very existence of the United States and Mexico. The northern part of the continent was settled by nomadic, warrior nations; Mesoamerica, on the other hand, was the home of an agricultural civilization, with complex social and political institutions, dominated by warlike theocracies that invented refined and cruel rituals, great art, and vast cosmogonies inspired by a very original vision of time. The great opposition of pre-Columbian America—all that now includes Canada, the United States, and Mexico—was not between distinct civilizations, as in the Ancient World, but between different ways of life: nomads and settled peoples, hunters and farmers. This division greatly influenced the later development of the United States and Mexico. The policies of the English and Spanish toward the American Indians were in large part determined by this fact: it was not insignificant that the former established themselves in the territory of the nomads and the latter in that of the settled peoples.

The differences between the Spaniards and the English who founded New Spain and New England were no less clearcut and decisive than those that separated the nomadic from the settled Indians. Again, it was an opposition within the same civilization. Just as the American Indians' world views and beliefs sprang from a common source, regardless of their ways of life, so the Spanish and English shared the same principles and the same intellectual and technical culture. And the opposition between them, though of a different sort, was as deep as that dividing an Aztec from an Iroquois. And so the new opposition between English and Spanish was grafted onto the old opposition between nomadic and settled peoples. The distinct and divergent attitudes of Spaniards and English have often been described before. Here I will only recall a fundamental difference, in which perhaps the dissimilar evolution of our countries originated: in England the Reformation triumphed, whereas Spain was the champion of the Counter Reformation.

As we all know, the reformist movement in England had political consequences that were decisive in the formation of Anglo-Saxon democracy. In Spain, evolution went the opposite way. Once the resistance of the last Muslims was crushed, Spain achieved a precarious political, but not national, unity by means of dynastic alliances. At the same time, the monarchy suppressed regional autonomies and municipal freedoms, closing off the possibility of eventual evolution to a modern democracy.

Finally, Spain was deeply marked by Arab domination and kept alive the notion of the crusade and the holy war, which she had inherited from Christian and Muslim alike. In Spain, the traits of the modern era that was just beginning and the traits of the old society coexisted but never blended completely. The contrast with England could not be sharper. The history of Spain and of her former colonies, from the sixteenth century onwards, is the history of our ambiguous relationship—attraction and repulsion—with the modern era. Even now, as modernity is waning, we are not completely modern.

The discovery and conquest of America are events that inaugurate modern history, but Spain and Portugal carried them out with the sensibility and tenor of the Reconquest. Nothing more original occurred to Cortés' soldiers, amazed by the pyramids and temples of the Mayans and Aztecs, than to compare them with the mosques of Islam. Conquest and evangelization: these two words, deeply Spanish and Catholic, are also deeply Islamic. Conquest did not mean only the occupation of foreign territories and the subjugation of their inhabitants; it meant also the conversion of the conquered. The conversion legitimized the conquest. This politico-religious philosophy was diametrically opposed to that of English colonizing; the idea of evangelization occupied a secondary place in England's colonial expansion.

The Spanish dominions were never really colonies in the traditional sense of the word. New Spain and Perú were viceroyalties, kingdoms subject to the crown of Castile, like the other Spanish kingdoms. On the other hand, the English settlements in New England and elsewhere were colonies in the classic sense. That is to say, they were communities established on foreign soil, preserving their cultural, religious, and political links with the mother country. This difference in attitude became combined with the difference in cultural conditions found by Spanish and English: nomadic and agricultural Indians, primitive societies and urban societies. The Spanish policy of subjection and conversion could not have been applied to the warlike Indian tribes of the North as easily as to the sedentary populations of Mesoamerica, as became clear a century later, when the Spanish conquest spread into the territory of the nomads, into what is today northern Mexico and the southern United States. The results of this double and contradictory set of circumstances were decisive. Without them, our countries would not be what they are.

The Spaniards wiped out the ruling classes of Mesoamerica, especially the priestly caste, which meant that they eliminated the memory of the conquered peoples. The aristocrats who escaped destruction were absorbed into the nobility, the church, and the bureaucracy. The Spanish policy toward the Indians had a double consequence: by reducing them to serfdom it turned them into cheap labor, so that they formed the basis of the hierarchical society of New Spain; at the same time, once they became Christians they survived both epidemics and servitude, and became a vital part of the future Mexican nation. The Indians were the backbone of Mexico, her first and last reality.

To racial crossbreeding we must add religious and cultural crossbreeding. The Christianity brought to Mexico by the Spaniards was the syncretic Catholicism of Rome, which had assimilated the pagan gods, turning them into saints and devils. The phenomenon was repeated in Mexico: the idols were baptized. In popular Mexican Catholicism the old beliefs and divinities are still present, barely hidden under a coating of Christianity. Not only the popular religion of Mexico but the Mexicans' entire life is steeped in Indian culture—the family, love, friendship, attitudes to one's father and mother, popular legends, the forms of politeness and life in common, the image of authority and political power, the vision of death and sex, work and festivity. Mexico is the most Spanish country in Latin America; at the same time, it is the most Indian. Mesoamerican civilization died a violent death, but Mexico is Mexico thanks to the Indian presence. Though the language and the religion, the political institutions and the culture of the country are Western, there is one side of Mexico that faces in another direction, the Indian direction. We are a nation between two civilizations and two pasts.

In the United States, the Indian component is not seen. This, in my opinion, is the major difference between our two

countries. In the United States, the Indians who were not exter-
minated were sequestered on "reservations." The Christian horror of "fallen nature" extended to the natives of North America;
the United States was founded on a land without an acknowl-
edged past. The historical memory of North Americans is European, not American. For this reason, one of the most powerful
and persistent directions of American literature, from Walt
Whitman to William Carlos Williams and from Herman Melville
to William Faulkner, has been the search for, or invention of,
American roots. We owe some of the major works of the modern
era to this impulse, this urgent desire for incarnation, this obses-
sive need to be rooted in American soil.

Exactly the opposite is true of Mexico, a land of superim-
posed pasts. Mexico City was built on the ruins of Mexico-
Tenochtitlán, the Aztec city, itself built in the likeness of Tula,
the Toltec city, built in the likeness of Teotihuacán, the first
great city on the American continent. Every Mexican bears
within him this continuity, which goes back two thousand years.
It does not matter that this presence is almost always uncon-
scious, and assumes the naive forms of legend and even supersti-
tion. It is not something known, but something *lived*. The Indian
presence means that one of the facets of Mexican culture is not
Western. Is there anything like this in the United States? Each of
the ethnic groups making up the multiracial democracy that is
the United States has its own culture and tradition, and some of
these—the Chinese and Japanese, for example—are not Western. These traditions exist alongside the central North American tradition without becoming one with it. They are foreign
bodies within North American culture. In some cases, the most
notable being that of the Chicanos, the minorities defend their
traditions against or in the face of the Anglo-American tradition. The Chicanos' resistance is cultural as well as political and
social.

If the different attitudes of Hispanic Catholicism and English Protestantism could be summed up in two words, I would
say that the Spanish attitude was *inclusive* and the English *exclusive*. In the former, the notions of conquest and domination are
bound up with ideas of conversion and assimilation; in the latter,

conquest and domination imply not the conversion of the conquered but his segregation. An inclusive society, founded on the
double principle of domination and conversion, was bound to be
hierarchic, centralist, and respectful of the individual characteristics of each group. It believed in the strict division of classes
and groups, each one governed by special laws and statutes, and
all believing in the same faith and obeying the same Lord.

An exclusive society was bound to cut itself off from the
natives, either by physical exclusion or extermination; at the
same time, since each community was an association of pure-
minded people and was isolated from other communities, it
tended to treat its members as equals, and to assure the autonomy and freedom of each group of believers. The origins of
Anglo-American democracy are religious, and in the early communities of New England that dual, contradictory tension between freedom and equality that has been the leitmotif of the
history of the United States is already present.

The opposition that I have just outlined is expressed with
great clarity in two religious terms: *communion* and *purity*. This
opposition profoundly affected attitudes toward work, festivity,
the body, and death. For the society of New Spain, work did not
redeem and had no value in itself. Manual work was servile. The
superior man neither worked nor traded: he made war, he com-
manded, he legislated. He also thought, contemplated, loved,
wooed, and enjoyed himself. Leisure was noble. Work was good
because it produced wealth, but wealth was good because it was
intended to be spent and consumed in those holocausts called
war, in the construction of temples and palaces, in pomp and
festivity. The dissipation of wealth took different forms: gold
shone on the altars or was poured out in festivities. Even today
in Mexico, at least in the small cities and towns, work is the
antechamber of the *fiesta*. The year revolves on the double axis
of work and festival, saving and spending. The *fiesta* is at once
sumptuous and intense, lively and funereal; it is a vital, mul-
ticolored frenzy that evaporates in smoke, ashes, nothingness. In
the aesthetics of perdition, the *fiesta* is the lodging place of death.

The United States has not really known the art of the festival, except in the last few years with the triumph of hedonism

over the old Protestant ethic. This is natural. A society that so energetically affirmed the redemptive value of work could not help but chastise as depraved the cult of the festival and the passion for spending. The Protestant condemnation was inspired by religion rather than economics. But the Puritan conscience could not see that the value of the festival was actually a religious value: communion. In the festival, the orgiastic element is central; it marks a return to the beginning, to the primordial state in which each one is united with the great All. Every true festival is religious because every festival is communion. Here the opposition between communion and purity is clear. For the Puritans and their heirs, work is redemptive because it is freeing, and this liberation is a sign of God's choice. Work is a purification that is also a separation: the chosen one ascends, breaking the bonds binding him or her to earth, namely, the laws of fallen nature. For the Mexicans, communion represents exactly the opposite: not separation but participation, not breaking away but joining together, the great universal commixture, the great bathing in the waters of the beginning, a state beyond purity and impurity.

In Christianity, the body's status is inferior. But the body is always an active force, and its explosions can destroy a civilization. Doubtless for this reason the church from the start made a pact with the body. If it did not restore the body to the place it had occupied in Greco-Roman society, at least the church did try to give the body back its dignity: the body is "fallen nature," but in itself it is innocent. After all, Christianity, unlike Buddhism, is the worship of an incarnate god. The dogma of the resurrection of the dead dates from the time of primitive Christianity; the cult of the Virgin appeared some time later and matured in the Middle Ages. Both beliefs are the highest expressions of the urge for incarnation that typifies Christian spirituality. Both came to Mesoamerica with Spanish culture and were immediately fused, the former with the funeral worship of the Indians, and the latter with the worship of the goddesses of fertility and war.

The Mexicans' vision of death, which is also the hope of resurrection, is as steeped in Catholic eschatology as it is in Indian naturalism. The Mexican death is of the body, exactly the opposite of the North American death, which is abstract and disembodied. For the Mexicans, death sees and touches itself; it is the body emptied of the soul, the pile of bones that somehow, as in the Aztec poem, must bloom again. For Anglo-Americans, death is what is not seen: absence, the disappearance of the person. In the Puritan consciousness, death was always present, but as an incorporeal presence, a moral entity, an idea. Later on, scientism pushed death out of the North American consciousness. Death melted away and became unmentionable. Finally, in vast segments of today's North American population, progressive rationalism and idealism have been replaced by neohedonism. But the cult of the body and of pleasure implies the recognition and acceptance of death. The body is mortal, and the kingdom of pleasure is that of the moment, as Epicurus saw better than anyone. North American hedonism closes its eyes to death, and has been incapable of exorcising the destructive power of the moment with a wisdom like that of the Epicureans of antiquity. Present-day hedonism knows no self-control. It is the last recourse of the anguished and the desperate, an expression of the nihilism that is eroding the West.

Capitalism exalts the activities and behavior patterns traditionally called virile: aggressiveness, the spirit of competition and emulation, combativeness. Anglo-American society made these values its own and exalted them. This perhaps explains why nothing like the Mexicans' devotion to the Virgin of Guadalupe appears in the different versions of Christianity professed by North Americans, including the Catholic minority. The Virgin unites the religious sensibilities of the Mediterranean with those of Mesoamerica, both regions that fostered ancient cults of feminine divinities. Guadalupe-Tonantzin is the mother of all Mexicans—Indians, mestizos, whites—but she is also a warrior virgin whose image has often appeared on the banners of peasant uprisings. In the Virgin of Guadalupe we encounter a very ancient vision of femininity that, as was true of the pagan goddesses, is not without a heroic tinge. It is what is called a "symbol incarnate," a presence.

Incidentally, when I talk about the "masculinity" of the North American capitalist society, I am not unaware that North American women have gained rights and positions still denied them elsewhere. But they have obtained them as "subjects under law," that is to say, as neuter or abstract entities, as citizens, not as women. I shall avoid this theme because, being predominantly political and social, it is not within the scope of these reflections. I will only say, in passing, that as much as equal rights for men and women, our civilization needs a "feminization" like the one that "courtly love" brought about in the mentality of medieval Europe, or an influence like the "feminine light" that the Virgin of Guadalupe casts on the imagination and sensibility of Mexicans.

Because of her Hispano-Arabic and Indian heritage, the social situation of the Mexican woman is deplorable—ours is the land of machismo—but what I want to emphasize here is not so much the nature of the relations between men and women as the intimate relationship of women to those elusive symbols that we call "femininity" and "masculinity." For the reasons I noted earlier, Mexican women have a very lively awareness of the body. For them the body, their own and the man's, is a concrete, palpable reality. Not an abstraction or a function, but an ambiguous magnetic force in which pleasure and pain, fertility and death, are inextricably intertwined.

Pre-Columbian Mexico was a mosaic of nations, tribes, and languages. For its part, Spain was also a conglomeration of nations and races, even though she had realized political unity. The heterogeneity of Mexican society was the other face of Spanish centralism. The political centralism of the Spanish monarchy had religious orthodoxy as its complement and even as its foundation. The true, effective unity of Mexican society has been brought about slowly over the course of several centuries, but its political and religious unity was decreed from above as the joint expression of the Spanish monarchy and the Catholic church. We had a state and a church before we were a nation. In this respect also our evolution has been very different from that of the United States, where the small colonial communities had from their inception a clear-cut and belligerent concept of their identity as regards the state. For the North Americans, the nation antedated the state.

Another difference is that in those communities a fusion of various factors had taken place—religious convictions, the embryonic national consciousness, and political institutions. As a result harmony, rather than contradiction, existed between the religious convictions of Anglo-Americans and their democratic institutions; whereas in Mexico, Catholicism was identified with the vice-regal regime and was its orthodoxy. Therefore, after independence, when the Mexican liberals tried to implant democratic institutions, they had to confront the Catholic church. The establishment of a republican democracy in Mexico meant a radical break with our past and led to the civil wars of the nineteenth century. These wars produced the militarism that in turn produced the dictatorship of Porfirio Díaz. The liberals defeated the church, but they could not implant true democracy, only an authoritarian regime wearing democracy's mask.

A third and no less profound difference was that between Catholic orthodoxy and Protestant reformism. In Mexico, Catholic orthodoxy had adopted the philosophical form of neo-Thomism, a mode of thought more apologetic than critical, and defensive in the face of the emerging modernity. Orthodoxy prevented examination and criticism. In New England, the communities were often made up of religious dissidents or at least of people who believed that the scriptures should be read freely. In an ideal sense, but not without exceptions, Catholic orthodoxy, dogmatic philosophy, and the cult of authority can be contrasted with Protestant flexibility and open interpretation of doctrine.

Both societies were religious, but their religious attitudes were irreconcilable. I am thinking not only of dogmas and principles, but also of the ways in which these societies practiced and understood religion. One society fostered the complex and majestic conceptual structure of orthodoxy, an equally complex ecclesiastic hierarchy, wealthy and militant religious orders like the Jesuits, and a ritualistic conception of religion in which the sacraments occupied a central place. The other fostered free discussion of the scriptures, a small and often poor clergy, a tendency to eliminate the hierarchic boundaries between the simple believer and the priest, and a religious practice based not on ritual but on ethics and not on the sacraments but on the internalization of faith.

If we consider the historical evolution of the two societies, the main difference seems to me to be the following: the modern world began with the Reformation, which was the religious criticism of religion, and the necessary antecedent of the Enlightenment; with the Counter Reformation and neo-Thomism, Spain and her possessions closed themselves to the modern world. We had no Enlightenment because we had neither a Reformation nor an intellectual religious movement like French Jansenism. And so, though Spanish-American civilization is to be admired on many counts, it reminds us of a construction of great solidity—at once convent, fortress, and palace—built to last, not to change. In the long run, that construction became a confine, a prison. The United States was born of the Reformation and the Enlightenment. It came into being under the sign of criticism and self-criticism. Today, when we talk of criticism we are talking of change. The transformation of critical philosophy into progressive ideology came about and reached its peak in the nineteenth century. The broom of rationalist criticism swept the ideological sky clean of myths and beliefs; in its turn, the ideology of progress displaced the timeless values of Christianity and transplanted them to the earthly and linear time of history. Christian eternity became the future of liberal evolutionism.

The difference I have just outlined is the final contradiction, and all the divergences and differences I have mentioned culminate in it. A society is essentially defined by its attitude toward time. Because of its origin and its intellectual and political history, the United States is a society oriented toward the future. The extraordinary spatial mobility of North America, a nation constantly on the move, has often been pointed out. In the realm of beliefs and mental attitudes, mobility in time corresponds to physical and geographic displacement. The North American lives on the very edge of the now, always ready to leap toward the future. The country's foundations are in the future, not the past. Or rather, its past, the act of its founding, was a promise for the future. Thus each time the United States returns to its source, to its past, it rediscovers the future.

Mexico's orientation, as we have seen, has been just the opposite. First came the rejection of criticism, and with it the notion of change: society's ideal is to conserve the image of divine immutability. Second, Mexican society has a plurality of pasts, all present and at war within every Mexican's soul. Cortés and Moctezuma are still alive in Mexico. At the time of that great crisis, the Mexican Revolution, the most radical faction, that of Zapata and his peasants, proposed no new forms of social organization but instead urged a return to communal ownership of land. The rebelling peasants were asking for the devolution of the land; that is, they wanted to go back to a pre-Columbian form of ownership that had been respected by the Spaniards. The image that the revolutionaries instinctively made for themselves of a golden age lay in the remote past. Utopia for them was not the construction of a future but a return to the source, to the beginning. The traditional Mexican attitude to time has been expressed in this way by a Mexican poet, Rámon López Velarde: "Motherland, be still the same, faithful to each day's mirror."

In the seventeenth century, Mexican society was richer and more prosperous than North American society. This situation lasted until the first half of the eighteenth century. To prove that it was so we need only glance at the cities of those days, with their monuments and buildings—Mexico City and Boston, Puebla and Philadelphia. In less than fifty years everything changed. In 1847, the United States invaded Mexico, occupied it, and imposed on it terrible and heavy conditions of peace. A century later, the United States became the first world power. An unusual conjunction of circumstances of a material, technological, political, ideological, and human order must be considered in explaining North America's prodigious development. Among these conditions, the set of attitudes I have briefly described was just as decisive as was the existence of a vast, rich territory, an enterprising population, and an extraordinary scientific and technological development. In the small religious communities of New England the future was already in bud; it was to be marked by political democracy, capitalism, and social and economic development. The United States' war of independence did not break with its past; the separation from England was not brought about to change the original principles for others but rather to achieve them more fully. In Mexico, the opposite occurred. At the end of the eighteenth century, the Mexican ruling classes—especially the intellectuals—discovered that the principles that had been the foundation of their society condemned it to immobility and backwardness. They undertook a twofold revolution: separation from Spain and modernization of the country through the adoption of new republican and democratic principles. Their examples were their neighbor's war of independence and the French Revolution. They gained independence from Spain, but the adoption of new principles was not enough; Mexico changed her laws, not her social, economic, and cultural realities.

During the first half of the nineteenth century, Mexico suffered a civil war and invasions by two foreign powers, the United States and France. In the second half of the century order was reestablished, but at the expense of democracy. The worst thing was that plague of Latin American societies—that in the name of liberal ideology and the positivism of Comte and Spencer, a military dictatorship was imposed and lasted thirty years. It was a period of peace and appreciable material development, and also one of increasing penetration by foreign, especially English and North American, capitalists. The Mexican Revolution of 1910 set itself the task of changing this direction. In part it succeeded. As this is one of the main themes of the symposium, I will not elaborate on it. I shall say only that Mexican democracy is not yet a reality, and that the great advances achieved in certain quarters have been nullified or are in danger because of excessive political centralization, exaggerated demographic growth, social inequality, the collapse of higher education, and the actions of the economic monopolies, among them the North American. As for our relationship with the United States, it is still the old relationship of strong and weak, oscillating between indifference and abuse, deceit and cynicism. Most Mexicans hold the understandable conviction that the treatment received by our country is unjust.

Above and beyond success and failure, the Mexico of today asks itself the same question that has occurred to most clear-thinking Mexicans ever since the end of the eighteenth century: How is modernization to be achieved? In the nineteenth century, we believed that it was enough to adopt new principles. Today, after almost two centuries of setbacks, we have realized that countries change very slowly, and that if such changes are to be fertile they must be in harmony with the past and with the tradition of each nation. Thus Mexico must find her own road to modernity. Our past must not be an obstacle but a starting point. This is extremely difficult, given the nature of our tradition—difficult, but not impossible. In fact this was the profound meaning of the Mexican Revolution. Long before us, Zapata's peasants took a last-ditch stand against modernization, and with arms. To avoid new disasters, we must reconcile ourselves with our past; only in this way shall we succeed in finding a path to modernity.

The search for our own model of modernization is a theme directly linked with another: today we know that modernity, both the capitalist and the pseudosocialist version practiced by the totalitarian bureaucracies, has a fatal flaw at its very center— the idea of continuous, unlimited progress. The nations that inspired our nineteenth-century liberals—England, France, and especially the United States—today are doubting, vacillating, and cannot find their way. They have ceased to be universal examples. The Mexicans of the nineteenth century turned their eyes toward the great Western democracies; we have nowhere to turn ours.

For more than thirty years, between 1930 and 1960, most Mexicans were sure of the path they had chosen. These certainties have vanished, and some people ask themselves if it may not be necessary to begin all over again. But the question is relevant not only for Mexico—it is universal. However unsatisfactory our country's situation may seem to us, it is not desperate, especially when compared with what prevails elsewhere. Latin America, with only a few exceptions, lives under military dictatorships

more or less pampered and often supported by the United
States. Cuba escaped American hegemony only to become a
pawn of the Soviet Union's policy of military aggression in Af-
rica. A large number of the Asian and African nations that
gained their independence after the Second World War are the
victims of native tyrannies often more cruel and despotic than
those of the old colonial powers. In the so-called Third World,
with different names and attributes, a ubiquitous "Caligula"
reigns.

In 1917, the October Revolution in Russia kindled the
hopes of millions; in 1978, the word *gulag* has become synony-
mous with Soviet socialism. The founders of the socialist movement firmly believed that socialism would put an end not only to
the exploitation of human beings but to war; in the second half
of the twentieth century, totalitarian "socialisms" have enslaved
the working class by stripping it of its basic rights—unionization
and the strike—and have involved the whole planet in the
threatening uproar of their disputes and quarrels. In the name
of different versions of "socialism," Vietnamese and Cambo-
dians butcher each other. The ideological wars of the twentieth
century are no less ferocious than the wars of religion.

When I was young, the idea that we were witnessing the
final crisis of capitalism was fashionable among intellectuals.
Now we understand that the crisis is not of a socioeconomic
system but of our whole civilization. It is a general, worldwide
crisis, and its most extreme, acute, and dangerous expression is
found in the situation of the Soviet Union and its satellites. The
contradictions of totalitarian "socialism" are more profound and
irreconcilable than those of the capitalist democracies.

The sickness of the West is moral rather than social and
economic. It is true that the economic problems are serious and
that they have not been resolved; on the contrary, inflation and
unemployment are on the rise. It is also true that poverty has not
disappeared; despite affluence, several groups—women, as well
as racial, religious, and linguistic minorities—still are or feel excluded. But the real, most profound discord lies in the soul. The
future has become the realm of horror, and the present has
turned into a desert. The liberal societies spin tirelessly, not

forward but round and round. If they change, they are not transfigured. The hedonism of the West is the other face of its desperation; its scepticism is not wisdom but renunciation; its nihilism ends in suicide and in inferior forms of credulity, such as political fanaticisms and magical chimeras. The empty place left by Christianity in the modern soul is not filled by philosophy but by the crudest superstitions. Our eroticism is a technique, not an art or a passion.

The evils of the West have been described often enough, most recently by Solzhenitsyn, a man whose spiritual vision is both sweeping and penetrating. I must say, however, that while his description seems to me accurate, his judgment of the causes of the sickness and the remedy he proposes are not. We cannot renounce the critical tradition of the West; nor can we return to the medieval, theocratic state. The dungeons of the Inquisition are not an answer to the *gulag* camps. It is not worthwhile to substitute the party-state for the church-state, one orthodoxy for another. The only effective weapon against orthodoxies is criticism, and in order to defend ourselves against the vices of intolerance and fanaticism our only recourse is the firm and lucid exercise of the opposing virtues of tolerance and freedom of spirit.

The crisis of the United States affects the very foundation of the nation, by which I mean the principles on which it was founded. I have already said that there is a leitmotif running throughout Anglo-American history, from the Puritan colonies of New England to our day—namely the tension between freedom and equality. The struggles of the blacks, the Chicanos, and other minorities are only an expression of this struggle. An external contradiction corresponds to this internal contradiction: the United States is a republic and an empire. In an essay I wrote several years ago, I pointed out that the first of these contradictions (the internal one between equality and freedom) was resolved in Rome by the suppression of freedom; Caesar's regime began as an egalitarian solution that, like all solutions by force, also ended in the suppression of equality. The other contradiction brought about the ruin of Athens, the first imperial republic in history.

It would be presumptuous on my part to propose solutions to this double contradiction. I think that every time a society finds itself in crisis it instinctively turns toward its origins and looks there for a sign, an indication, if not a response. Colonial Anglo-American society was a free, egalitarian, but exclusive society. Faithful to its origins, in its domestic and foreign policies alike, the United States has always ignored the *other*. On the inside are the blacks, the Chicanos, and the Puerto Ricans; on the outside are the marginal cultures and societies. Today the United States faces very powerful enemies, but the mortal danger comes from within, not from Moscow but from that mixture of arrogance and opportunism, blindness and short-term Machiavellianism, volubility and stubbornness that have characterized its foreign policies during recent years and that remind us in an odd way of the Athenian state in its quarrel with Sparta. To conquer its enemies, the United States must first conquer itself—return to its origins. Not to repeat them, but to rectify them: the *other* and the others—the minorities inside, as well as the marginal countries and nations outside—do exist. Not only do we make up the majority of the human race, but also each marginal society, poor though it may be, represents a unique and precious version of humanity. These are serious times. If the United States is to recover integrity and lucidity, it must recover itself, and to recover itself it must recover the others— the outcasts of the Western world.

PART 1

THE PEOPLE AND CULTURE OF MEXICO

The Roots of Mexican Culture

Ignazio Bernal

We can trace the beginnings of Mexican culture back to about 1200 B.C., when signs of civilization appeared among the people we call the Olmecs, who lived in the area that is now Veracruz. Among the Olmecs, we see evidence of careful urban planning, the first preconceived system of where buildings should be placed. In the case of La Venta, the city was divided in half by a north-south axis, along which the principal monuments were constructed. These enormous sculptures were in themselves outstanding evidence of civilization—they were carved from tremendous blocks of stone that had been carried from great distances to the Olmecs' Gulf Coast homeland, where such stone is nonexistent.

Thus, with the Olmecs, great art appears for the first time on the American continent, and this fact, coupled with other knowledge we have of these people, tells us that in the Olmec civilization a relatively dense population lived within a small area. This denser demography brought with it a series of economic and political problems that could not be solved by the old tribal or magical systems that had previously been in use. The simple agriculture of small communities was no longer enough, and new means of supplying the people's needs, based fundamentally on trade, began to appear.

Today, we often think of commerce as an activity that flourishes in times of peace. However, I believe that the

Mesoamerican commerce that began with the Olmecs had nothing to do with peace. Rather, it was linked to war: the Olmecs traded with people who had been dominated, or at least intimidated, by force.

The Olmec world expanded in other areas as well—particularly in religious ceremonialism, perhaps the clearest reference point in the native world. In Olmec times, religion began to grow increasingly complex, placing more demands on the believer, its ceremonies becoming more and more associated with certain mental attitudes. In time, these became part not only of the religious world, but also of the civilization as a whole, as ritual forms entered even the simplest acts of daily life.

Although the Olmecs, for reasons we do not yet know, had declined in influence by about 400 B.C., another great and more broadly based culture arose as their successor. We call this Teotihuacán, for the capital and principal city of that name that is still visible in the immense ruins twenty-five miles from present-day Mexico City. With the emergence of Teotihuacán, the Mexican highlands, previously a peripheral region, became the cultural, economic, political, and religious center of Mesoamerica.

We can see many Olmec influences at Teotihuacán. For example, even the plan of the great city itself, with the Avenue of the Dead, the original axis that runs from north to south, follows the customary Olmec pattern. To this, however, is added a new element: the main avenue is bisected by a transverse axis running from east to west, forming an immense cross that divides the city into separate quarters.

It was not only in urban planning that Teotihuacán followed the Olmec tradition. When the city grew (at its height, in the seventh century, it had more than 200,000 inhabitants, making it one of the largest cities in the world), the agriculture of the Valley of Mexico and the Valley of Puebla was not sufficient to feed all its people, not to mention those living in the many towns and villages nearby. Teotihuacán had, therefore, to find another means of supplying its needs—and it did so exactly as the Olmecs had, by an imperial type of expansion, following the Olmec example in economic, commercial, and military matters, as well as in the collection of tribute. Expeditions were sent to distant lands, and merchants returned from these conquered territories with new products not found in the highlands—chocolate, cotton, quetzal feathers, and jade.

Teotihuacán had all the urban features that we use to define a civilization: a range of social classes, from the most menial laborers through intermediate groups to the highest leaders; professional people dedicated to specialized occupations; and an organized religion with gods, an established ceremonial, a fixed form of worship repeated on appropriate days of the year, and a professional priesthood. The appearance of the professional priesthood is particularly important: the priest is no longer the magician of ancient times; instead he becomes a figure dedicated to religion who has studied to reach his position, a man recognized as holding all knowledge.

The monumental art first seen among the Olmecs also continued, joined by the development of mural painting and the production of an enormous variety of vessels and decorative objects. Some of these were produced for use in the great city and others were for export, providing the basis for trade with other areas.

By any standards, the civilization of Teotihuacán was an immense success, and from this it derives its fundamental importance in terms of the Mexican destiny. With Teotihuacán, the central highland valleys replaced the lowlands and coastal areas of the Olmecs as the geopolitical center of Mesoamerica. From this period, the center of power would be found in the valleys of Mexico and Puebla.

Around A.D. 650, the city of Teotihuacán was plundered and burned. But while Teotihuacán was destined to disappear, its achievements were not. The best known of its heirs and successors were the Toltecs, who established their capital at Tula in the same central highland region. With the Toltecs, we have the appearance of the first historical figure of ancient Mexico, Quetzalcoatl, who was elevated to the status of a hero-god. This illustrious man figures deeply in the Toltecs' history, but even more so in their legends. According to Toltec tradition, Quetzal-coatl was the inventor of agriculture, medicine, and the calendar; the first to use written language; the discoverer of the path of the sun, moon, and stars; the founder of royalty. In short, all progress was due to Quetzalcoatl. Of course, the discoveries attributed to him were really made long before his time, which gives the Toltec empire the flavor of a posthumous creation. But if nothing else, the Toltecs are important, in my opinion, because they carried on the thread of history and managed to pass it to their own heirs, serving as the link between Teotihuacán and what would later become the Aztec capital.

The Mexica, whom we incorrectly call the Aztecs, were an insignificant people who rose to power in the twelfth century, taking over all they could hold of the ancient heritage. In fact, they were so anxious to be considered descendants of the Toltecs that at the time of their triumph their leader took a title that means "Lord of the Toltecs." By this, the Mexica meant to signify not only their possession of the Toltec empire, but also the direct descent of their emperor from Quetzalcoatl.

In designing their capital, Tenochtitlán, the Mexica repeated the pattern of Teotihuacán, but on a smaller scale, building four main avenues that intersected to form a cross, with a great temple in the center. Again, the city was divided into quarters, and each of these subdivided into wards. These wards, or *calpullis* in Nahuatl, preserved two elements of the old tribal life. Only people born within the *calpulli* belonged to it and were therefore related to its other members. To this idea of a physical type of kinship was added the communal ownership of land: only members of the *calpulli* could use its lands, which were parceled out among the inhabitants according to need. Above the *calpulli* organization was the imperial government that ruled the city and the many tributary provinces. The emperor or *tlacatecuhtli*, was head of the government and held extensive power.

The *calpulli* is a particularly interesting aspect of Mexica society because it casts light on certain facets of modern Mexican life. In a similar way, the great development of language and protocol that occurred in the Mexica period is also relevant to modern Mexico. Nahuatl is a language rich in expressions of affability and courtesy, in long moral discourses that are presented on many occasions. This produced a highly verbal culture in which great importance was placed on speaking well and abiding by established formulas.

A final influence that can be traced back to the Mexica stems from its terrible religion, which demanded human sacrifice. The Mexica had taken upon themselves the appalling task of supplying their god, the sun, with nourishment to keep it alive, and the sun fed only on human blood. I believe that the tremendous death complex so often shown in Mexican art and life derives from this period.

Let us now turn to the other side of Mexico's inheritance, the Spanish influence that arrived with Cortés. Clearly, the character and individuality of Spanish life comes from its mosaic of different cultures. However, because so little has survived of the aboriginal culture of the region, the Roman heritage and that of Visigoth Christianity form the two pillars of the Spanish world. But these were not the only influences on Spanish life. For seven centuries, Islam totally or partially dominated the region, leaving an indelible impression on its culture. The Jewish influence upon the life and thought of medieval Spain also left its mark. Thus, sixteenth-century Spain was a reflection of the entire Mediterranean world, uniting the Roman, Moorish, and Jewish cultures with that of Christianity.

The Hispanic impact was felt not so much during the Conquest as during the colonization that followed—and in the way that colonization was carried out. The native religion, and the whole ritual world associated with it, was supplanted, but at the same time the general organization of the native empire continued. It is interesting to see how much of Moctezuma was carried over in the viceroys. Indeed, the presidents of independent Mexico still continue that image in the *caudillo*, the political boss who plays a much more individual than institutional role. The government is centered in a man who has all-embracing powers, exactly as Moctezuma did. Even now, the president is surrounded by a narrow circle of intimates and friends reminiscent of that of the Aztec *tlacatecuhtli.*

But I am getting ahead of my story. In the early days of the Conquest, and in the years that followed, there was no sense that all these influences would fuse to form a Mexican identity. In the latter half of the seventeenth century, some illustrious souls, such as Sor Juana Inés de la Cruz and Don Carlos de Sigüenza y Góngora, anticipated the idea of nationality, speaking of Mexico and things Mexican. In the case of Sor Juana, these references were merely elements of her courtly poetry, dedicated to the viceroys and their wives—hardly expressions of incipient nationalism. But Sigüenza presents a more complex and important development. Born in Veracruz of Spanish parents, he spent much time and effort in collecting and studying native antiquities. When he was commissioned to erect a triumphal arch to welcome the viceroy in 1680, he departed from the custom of the time by using Aztec emperors as decorations rather than figures of classical mythology. In his expressions of love for his country, Sigüenza is a prelude to the new culture, embodying a reverence for the past without thinking in terms of political independence.

In my opinion, the true Mexican originated in the eighteenth century with the scholarly group whose leading member, Francisco Javier Clavijero, was a Jesuit. At the time, the European Encyclopedists were presenting the idea that life degenerates in the Americas—plants become unfruitful, animals are born smaller, individuals are dull-witted, lakes become salty, and so on. Infuriated, Clavijero presented his arguments against this position in his well-known work, *The Ancient History of Mexico,* a defense not only of its physical world, but also a demonstration of the ancient grandeur of its native peoples.

The New World had still other reasons for heightened self-awareness. Although many eminent citizens were profoundly influenced by the Enlightenment (and the new French culture would serve at least to alienate them partially from the traditional Spanish culture), they still found that European scholars rejected or ignored their achievements. In their own defense, denizens of the New World would themselves have to provide evidence of the value of their culture. In the process, such authors as Juan José de Eguiara and Juan Luis Maneiro came to consider "culture" to be the same as "nationality." With these men, the question was posed for the first time: They say we are not Spaniards. And we are not Indians. So what are we? The answer—we are Mexicans—would begin a tradition that would inevitably lead to independence.

Thus a national consciousness and an independent culture were formed. And from the need to encourage and protect them arose the impetus to study the native world and preserve its antiquities. The viceroy himself gave orders to protect the great pieces of Aztec art that were found in the main plaza of Mexico City in 1790. Thanks to him, the Sun Stone (the Aztec calendar), Coatlicue, and the monument to the victories of Tizoc were preserved. These and other artifacts were described in writing a short time later by Antonio de León y Gama, the first Mexican archaeologist.

Lack of space prevents me from discussing the nineteenth century and the strong influences on Mexico from both the United States and France. In any case, it is easy to see in modern Mexican culture the influences that come to us from both North America and Europe. What are less clear are the many traits of the native, pre-Hispanic civilization that have survived into the present. An enormous list of these elements, now accepted as part of the character of Mexico as a nation, could be composed, but for now let us confine ourselves to several interesting examples.

Consider for a moment Mexico's daily diet: turkey and tortillas, peanuts and chocolate, red and green chili peppers, the avocado and guava, herbs for seasoning, not to mention the whole variety of maize products. All these come from the native culture of pre-Columbian times. In the same way, utensils such as the *metate* for grinding corn, the *comal* for baking tortillas, lacquered gourds, and countless other items found in many Mexican homes were also used in pre-Hispanic times.

Consider also the language spoken in Mexico, which, as we all know, differs in many ways from that of Spain. Many words of native origin have become part of our everyday vocabulary, although they have been adapted to Spanish forms. In addition, different meanings are sometimes given to Spanish words. For example, in Mexico the words *parate* ("stop") and *levantate* ("get up") are used interchangeably, while in Spanish, as in English, they are two completely different verbs. Why? Because in Nahuatl only one verb is used to indicate both actions. In other words, we are using Spanish but applying a Nahuatl meaning.

Very often we also alter the semantics and even the pronunciation of words. For instance, diminutives *(ahorita, luegito, ratito)* come from that native world of affability that decreases the size of an object to make it sound more pleasing. And this brings us to the typically indigenous use of courtesies such as "my home is your home" and "please command me," all foreign to the blunt directness of the Spaniard. At the same time, though, this courtesy often masks a violence that is related to the Mexicans' well-known machismo and their exaltation of death, a complex that has its origins in the Aztec concept of the world beyond the grave. Perhaps the habit of giving people nicknames that refer to physical defects also falls within this same order of ideas.

Another present-day link with pre-Hispanic Mexico is the *ejido*, whose resemblance to the indigenous *calpulli* was mentioned earlier. Another example is the Mexican market, which is entirely different from markets in other parts of the world, not in what is sold but in the way the merchandise is distributed. There is a section for vegetables, a section for shoes, another for pottery, and so forth—just as it was in the market at Tenochtitlán.

As a matter of fact, if we look at maps of the great colonial cities—Mexico City, Puebla, and Oaxaca, for example—we can see that not only their markets but their entire layout is indigenous. The arrangement of church-palace-plaza-market is a typical Teotihuacán and Mexica combination, very different from the arrangement seen in medieval Spanish cities. And finally we find in the Mexican capital itself—located at 7,244 feet above sea level in a valley that is not especially fertile—the direct result of the triumph achieved by Teotihuacán as the axis of the ancient world. The country has continued to be governed from the same place for more than two thousand years.

It is easy to see, then, that Mexico has a dual heritage. And while the descent from two civilizations has been a fundamental problem, it has also been Mexico's glory, giving her a culture different from all others and, even more important, giving her the possibility for independent survival.

The Beginning of a Nation: The Nineteenth Century

Josefina Vásquez

Who are the Mexican people? How did this nation come about? How can you define us? How can we define ourselves? I have always been concerned about these difficult questions. I often notice that other people look at us and see that we can be distinguished from others, yet when I see people living in Mexico, when I travel in Mexico, I see a great variety of types, a great variety of customs, a great variety of ways of speaking. In spite of everything, we have become a nation. And to the extent that we are, it is a result of the image of nationhood held by the Creoles who won independence and had a dream of making a separate country against great odds.

There were two great obstacles to making a nation in what is now Mexico. One is geographical. When we look at a map of Mexico, we see much yellow and brown, the colors that represent mountains, and scarcely any green, which indicates that there is very little water. This has created difficulties because it means that the country is made up of isolated valleys with poor communication among them. Historically, these conditions have resulted in small, very close-knit cultural groups that communicated with one another but still kept very much to themselves.

The other obstacle is the human one. We are the result of

the mingling of three different groups—whites, Indians, and blacks—in a diversity of proportions. In central Mexico, along the highlands, the population is mainly mestizo; there are isolated pockets of almost pure Indians in certain areas; in others there are other proportions of ethnic groups, with a larger component of blacks.

History and a common historical experience have been a bridge past these obstacles. The Conquest, the main reason for Mexico's existence, is the general link. In a practical way, the Conquest made the different Indian cultures dependent on one government, that of Spain, for over three centuries. This experience becomes even more important when it is considered in terms of Christianization, the spiritual conquest that followed the military one. While not many Indians learned to speak Spanish, most were Christianized in some fashion.

The significance of the religious factor could be seen in 1821, at the time of independence, when the country still had a great proportion of Indians. About 60 or 70 percent of the population were Indians; only 10 percent were whites, Creoles, or Peninsulares; and the others were a mingling of the different races. The Creoles dreamed of making Mexico an independent nation, but they knew that it would be difficult to rule over so many different groups. In an effort to unify the people, to make them feel that they had a common future as well as a common past, most Creoles turned to the power of the Church. Because they saw that the only natural tie they had was the Catholic religion, they were not prepared to tolerate any other faith.

The Creoles also believed that the two most important ways of developing the nation would be education—making the people feel that they were Mexicans and teaching them what being a Mexican meant—and developing communication with the isolated areas of the country in order to bring groups into closer contact with one another so that they would become more and more alike. Through all of our national history, our government has been trying to accomplish both these tasks. This is why we have a rather special way of seeing the educational process, one that North Americans very often do not understand.

While these programs have been, in a way, quite successful,

it is also true that history itself has helped to unify our pluralistic society. For this reason, I would like to touch briefly on some events in the nineteenth century, a century that is so little understood and yet so important in the making of the Mexican nation.

For half of the nineteenth century, Mexico's history was quite dramatic: internal convulsions, instability, the threat of other countries trying to take our resources or our territory. We had to defend ourselves constantly. Yet both the instability of Mexican society and the intervention of foreign countries worked to our advantage because the kind of identity that emerged from them was in the long run more important than the losses that were suffered.

The armies provide a good example of just how this identity was forged. Admittedly, conscription was a terrible institution, one of the greatest burdens on the people of nineteenth-century Mexico, but it forced Indians and mestizos from the rural areas to enter the army and fight in other parts of the country. Conscription made it possible for people who did not speak Spanish to learn Spanish and to become acquainted with other regions. In a sense, it made them Mexicans.

Of course, at the time of independence those who ruled the country, the Creoles, were aware of their inheritance and were proud of their history. But the common people really were not. They were illiterate. They were isolated. They found it difficult to change loyalties suddenly from the king to the republic and to have a different view of themselves. For this reason, the wars we had to fight with other countries, especially with the United States and with France, helped these people know what it meant to be Mexican.

At the time of the first intervention by U.S. troops, the reaction of the Mexican populace was simply one of curiosity. Common people came to Puebla in 1848 just to see the North American soldiers. Mexicans had heard many stories about these soldiers, and at first they did not react to them with hostility. They did not understand the threat because they were not aware of their nationhood. However, after the people had experienced the presence of foreign troops in Mexico, they realized all too well what was involved. It was a terrible but a very practical lesson, one whose results can be seen in the quite different reaction shown to the French troops that arrived about twenty years later. When the second invasion occurred, it was easier to mobilize the people to defend their country. In a way, they had learned what Mexico meant.

After the second foreign intervention in 1867, the government was able to develop the two main roads to unity—communications and education. Of course, neither has been an easy task: the mountainous terrain is difficult to tame and everything is costly. It is also very difficult to convince people to adopt new ideas. But if you compare what we are today as a nation—how we feel about ourselves and the way we have been able to work together—with what we were at the beginning of the nineteenth century, then it is obvious that the dream of the people who made Mexico has succeeded in a very great way.

Nation-Building in the Twentieth Century

Rodolfo Stavenhagen

The story we read in textbooks about Mexico is the story of what in modern political and sociological terms is called nation-building. This is a long historical process, one that all countries have gone through, although in different stages and in different ways. Certainly the United States has gone through it, and so has Mexico.

What does nation-building mean? In the economic and social areas, it means modernization, to employ another commonly used term. Modernization involves the establishment of industry and a modern mercantile commercial economy; the breaking down of the natural subsistence economy; and the changeover from a population made up mainly of peasants and agriculturists to a population made up mainly of workers in the industrial or secondary sector and in trades and services—in other words, the rise of the so-called middle class. In the cultural field, nation-building means, as Bernal and Vásquez have pointed out in the previous chapters, a process of unification, a process of cultural homogenization.

All of these processes have taken place in Mexico, but only to a certain extent. This is true, in part, because the very act of nation-building has created its own obstacles. In this chapter, I would like to discuss briefly the factors that have made the task of economic and social modernization more difficult.

We should begin by recognizing the fact that even today, after many years of economic development, after sixty years of social revolution, up to 40 percent of Mexico's labor force is still concentrated in agriculture. In other words, we have not yet been able to undertake the revolutionary step that is usually considered to be part and parcel of modernization—that is, to improve our agricultural productivity and decrease the number of people who actually labor in agriculture in order to provide the nonagricultural sectors with labor.

This failure can be traced to a very complex set of historical and structural forces that are, unfortunately, beyond the scope of this chapter. However, the basic fact is that the kind of economic growth, the kind of industrialization, that has been seen in Mexico for the last thirty-five or forty years, the so-called "take-off" years, has not been able to absorb enough labor to produce basic changes in the occupational structure. As a result, we still have a large number of people in agriculture, a very high rate of unemployment and underemployment, and a very high rate of migration to the United States. The hundreds of thousands of migrant laborers, many of them undocumented, who come into the United States every year from Mexico are forced to do so as a result of the structural aspects of the Mexican economy.

Because of this situation, it is likely that for many more years millions of people in Mexico will be employed in agriculture. We will have peasants, millions of peasants. I use the word "peasants" because this is not, except in a few cases and for a minority of the population, a modern, commercially oriented, highly technological agriculture. Rather, for most of these people it is a small-scale, almost self-sufficient, technologically low-level subsistence economy. And for many more, it means being part of a landless rural labor force. On the basis of research and statistical analysis, I would estimate that about 70 percent of the labor force in Mexican agriculture today consists of the poorest of the poor peasants, with very low-level technology and productivity—which means, in turn, a very low level of income and a very low standard of living.

Another troublesome aspect of nation-building has to do

with cultural unification. As Vásquez has pointed out, the nineteenth century was characterized by a heroic effort, one that has continued into the twentieth century—the effort to build a national identity. In Mexico, this movement ran into two basic obstacles.

The first was the attacks on Mexico by foreign nations during the nineteenth century, a period in which the country was prey to proponents of "Manifest Destiny." During what in the United States is called the Mexican-American War (but which we call the North American Intervention), Mexico lost half of her territory. There was also a French intervention, as well as an Austrian emperor on the Mexican throne. In sum, there were strong pressures from the French, the Germans, the British, and the North Americans. Thus the Mexican elite of the nineteenth century, and the Mexican nation as a whole, did not simply imagine the danger of foreign attack. If one reads public North American statements of the period, Mexico is always mentioned as a possible protectorate, arguments are made constantly as to why the United States should conquer Mexico.

The modernizing elite in Mexico recognized that in order to strengthen the nation against foreign interests, whether in the form of direct military intervention or of political and economic interests, it was necessary to strengthen the nation internally. Another obstacle to this unification was the existence in Mexico of a number of culturally distinct groups, a number of different languages. In other words, the existence of non-Spanish-speaking, non-Mexican-feeling Indian groups was considered as much an obstacle to nation-building as external threats. Therefore, ever since the nineteenth century, government policy—through social modernization, social investment, and particularly educational policy—has tended toward the cultural unification of the country, which in practice means the disappearance of minority ethnic groups. In recent decades, this has meant a conscious policy of assimilation or integration of Indians. In other words, the existence of mainly peasant communities in backward, isolated rural areas, the existence of people who did not speak the national language and who did not take part in the national economy as such, was considered a

serious obstacle to the strengthening of the nation vis-à-vis
foreign interests. In this way, external relations and the need for
economic modernization are directly related to cultural policy in
Mexico.

Yet what has happened? Just as the peasants have not disappeared despite the best intentions of economic planners, so the
Indians have not disappeared despite efforts at cultural
homogenization, integration, and assimilation through educational means. Today, over fifty different distinct linguistic
groups are still very much alive in Mexico. For example, the
state of Oaxaca is a fabulously rich mosaic of different Indian
groups, with Zapotecs and Mixtecs predominating among
another million and a half speakers of indigenous languages.
Thus by the latest census information (which is probably an
underestimation), Mexico has five or six million non-Spanish-
speaking citizens, a group that makes up between 10 and 15
percent of the population, mainly in rural areas. And there is,
furthermore, a strong statistical correlation between backward
peasant communities and linguistically and culturally distinct
Indian communities.

What does this mean for the future? What is the government's policy regarding both peasants and Indian groups? The
economic development strategy of the last few decades has not
been able either to break the peasant economy or to make the
Indians disappear. Since the peasant economy has resulted in a
marginal existence for millions of people in the urban areas, a
strategic question for planners is what can be done, not to make
the peasant economy disappear, but to strengthen it at the present stage of Mexico's development so that millions of peasants
can raise their standard of living. At the same time, another
question is posed in the cultural sphere. Is there still a need for
the complete assimilation of Indians into the national fabric in
order for Mexico to become a strong nation? Or has Mexico
already come so far that the country can well afford to allow a
certain number of minorities to maintain their ethnic and cultural identity?

Indeed, there is a kind of cultural movement occurring in
Mexico today in which different Indian groups have become

vocal in defending their right to maintain their own distinct cultural and linguistic identity in the face of modernization. They argue effectively and convincingly that in order to be "good" Mexicans (whatever that may mean) it is not necessary either to lose their various indigenous identities or the use of their own languages. It is now recognized in Mexican government circles (in the Ministry of Education, in the National Indian Institute, in other organizations, and among the intellectual elites) that Mexico remains a multicultural community—that we can be a strong nation with a clear identity, a nation conscious of its historical past as well as its future, and yet not deny cultural minorities their right to their own identity.

There is at present, then, a change in attitude taking place in Mexico. A policy that derived from the nineteenth century, one of assimilation and incorporation in order to create a culturally homogeneous nation, is being replaced by a policy based on the fact of an existing nation-state, the dangers to which have largely disappeared, that maintains a tolerant approach to ethnic groups. Mexico has today, and probably will continue to have for several decades to come, a large peasant population that is, in a way, marginal to the process of economic modernization and that will not be absorbed by this process. At the same time, the existence of this peasant population—very poor, with a very low standard of living, and very isolated—is directly related to the existence of distinct Indian groups. The sacrifice of modernization for one will, in effect, be a prime factor in the preservation of the other.

PART 2

THE MEXICAN STATE

The Revolution, the Constitution, and the Progress of the Mexican State

Porfirio Muñoz Ledo

These essays dedicated to the land and people of Mexico mark the beginning of a project whose timeliness and scope should not be ignored—they are an attempt to bring to the nerve centers of the North American community those images and words that best reflect what is presently occurring in another part of the world.

It has been said that the United States has attained its international responsibilities as a result of its economic expansion rather than as a result of a preconceived political plan. Thus its main duty has been to preserve the means of production and even the ways of life that brought about its prosperity, something that has rarely been compatible with an understanding of other points of view. For generations there has been a natural tendency among U.S. citizens to believe that their country's own experiences can be reproduced on an international scale. As a nation, the United States was able to forge together the contributions of the widest variety of races and cultures. Nevertheless, it should also be noted that a spiritual pluralism lies deep in the innermost recesses of this nation and that in spite of their uniformity in terms of technology or political dogma all the countries of the world have unique cultures.

To understand others involves more than the collection of

data. Today, North America has the most developed sources of information on what is happening abroad. Yet this does not necessarily imply a better understanding. On the whole, useful knowledge is gathered together to ease decision-making rather than to gain awareness. We should ask ourselves if the arbitrary use of this data by mass media and interest groups in the United States has led to a heightening of prejudices regarding other groups of people and has interfered with healthy relationships with other nations. In the case of Mexico, one cannot deny that this has taken place.

Our relationship as neighbors is a peculiar one. Despite centuries of close physical proximity, despite the intense contacts established during recent decades, and despite the millions of Mexicans who have joined in the efforts of the United States, we now discover that in reality we are strangers. Today the most clear-sighted citizens of the United States comprehend that among their countrymen there still prevails a stereotypic view— be it aggressive or paternalistic—of what we Mexicans are. This volume of essays seeks to contribute to a transformation of this situation, to emerge with understanding rather than mistrust.

In spite of numerous studies, the Mexican political system continues to be misunderstood by many foreign analysts. In other words, it seems that it has not been possible to overcome the ethnocentric attitude according to which political life in other parts of the globe is judged on the basis of the particular tradition and values of the observer. Thus, in offering a Mexican view of my country's political system, I should like to discuss a few fundamental ideas that are related to the system's approach rather than simply describe the workings of the system itself. After all, political institutions form a living part of a culture. If we are to understand them, we must know why they were established, what their historical role has been, and what types of challenges they have had to confront.

The Mexican political system is the product of a long and painful struggle through which we have sought to shape our nationality. That is its foremost distinctive trait. In Mexico, the state was not originally the product of an established nation but rather the means with which to build such a nation. Our political institutions were not organized for the purpose of protecting the freedoms or property of a chosen few; instead, they were designed to make freedom and prosperity possible for all by changing society.

In his essay, Octavio Paz has pointed out the contrast between our experience and that of the United States. In Mexico, when we parted ways with Spain, we discovered that the principles that had governed our life as a colony were condemning us to immobility, and thus we were forced to undertake a lengthy revolution in order to modify ideas, customs, and forms of ownership. On the other hand, the Revolutionary War in the United States succeeded in breaking down the barriers that prevented the formation of a modern community. In Mexico those barriers were left untouched by the independence movement, for their roots were stronger and they were not conquered by either political or military means. This accounts for the nature— both violent and markedly ideological—of the political confrontation that occurred in our emerging nation, a battle between two realities and two opposing views of life. But it also explains the fact that the solutions arrived at later were, after all, a synthesis of our indigenous and colonial traditions with programs geared toward change, of age-old Mexico and a society open to that which is modern.

Colonial rule in Mexico was characterized by an assumption of native servitude and a determination to instill a political and religious order. It encountered numerous indigenous civilizations with political organizations that were basically tribal and theocratic, with a center of power in what is now Mexico City. On top of the preexisting ways of life, the colonial rulers imposed new ones, and for centuries our country preserved an unjust balance between Spaniards, Creoles, Indians, and a growing population of mestizos.

At the beginning of the nineteenth century, Mexico felt a need to define a new plan for the nation, and in doing so its leaders turned to the ideas and liberal institutions of the Western world. Gradually, Mexico adopted the ones that best met its needs: to oppose a society made up of castes, it chose legal equality; to oppose a concentration of wealth, small property; to oppose obscurantism, freedom of thought; to oppose the power of the Church, secular control; to oppose political centralizaton, federalism; and to oppose colonial domination, a stress on nationalism. It took Mexico half a century of armed strife to ensure that these new ideas would rise above the old and that the social forces upholding them would defeat the conservative ones, achieving a widespread consensus. Moreover, during this process we endured two military invasions, in one of which we lost the greater part of our territory and found ourselves unable to develop our productive forces.

The generations that fought for the triumph of democratic institutions were unable to put them into practice because the transmission of power from one party to another was invariably effected by armed force. Political participation was spirited, and the ideological and parliamentary debates noteworthy, but the instability that prevailed for so long made it impossible for democracy to be exercised on a regular basis.

The victory of Juárez secured the internal and external sovereignty of the state. At the same time, it meant a reconquering of our territory, confidence in our capability as a nation, and the establishment of a strong and respected constitution. Nevertheless, by the 1870s we had not yet managed to bring about essential changes in the economic and social structures we had inherited from the colonial period. Out of this contradiction came a lengthy dictatorship similar to all those that, in the name of progress, continue to promote the prosperity of limited sectors of the population at the expense of the majority.

The contrast between a republican form of government and a de facto authoritarian state highlighted the huge gap between the modern facade displayed by the country's upper classes and what a clever North American journalist termed "barbarous" Mexico, submerged in ancestral backwardness. In 1910 there was a rebellion against this "enlightened bossism" by a coalition of the middle classes, whose liberal expectations were thwarted by political rigidity and economic feudalism, and the forgotten working people in both the countryside and the cities.

The Mexican Revolution was not a mere bourgeois revolution within the Western tradition. It was a social revolution as well, the first of its kind during this century. In it were expressed the claims of small property owners in opposition to the monopolies and the great landed estates; those of democratic consciences in opposition to political oppression; those of Mexican owners in opposition to foreign companies; those of the workers in opposition to unjust working conditions; and those of the peasants, mestizos, and Indians in opposition to the usurpation of their land and their rights. Thus, during the first decade of this century, Mexico was stirred, for the first time, throughout its entire territory, and the social currents put into motion took several years to find their course. Finally, in 1917, our country defined the basis of the political system by which it has been governed ever since.

The Mexican Constitution is an exceptional document, the first one to go well beyond the conception of the liberal state and outline a set of institutions and principles for the independent development of a country that belongs to what we now call the Third World. To understand our institutions is, above all, to understand the Constitution that brought them into being and what it means in terms of historical synthesis and national ideology—the principles that inspire it, the objectives it seeks to fulfill, and the mechanisms it has established to achieve its goals.

In Mexico freedoms neither come before nor are superior to the Constitution. Rather, they are spheres of action that this supreme law grants and guarantees. Based on this idea, an active state is defined in a different way from the concept formed by the liberals in the nineteenth century—it is responsible forthe fulfillment of certain goals that will assure national autonomy and promote social justice. Thus, in addition to the traditional charter of individual rights, the Mexican Constitution also includes social rights for workers, peasants, and their organizations, with both kinds of rights—individual and social—considered as *human* rights. In addition, it recognizes that the nation, represented by the state, has original rights involving land, water, and natural resources and grants the nation authority to prevent an excessive concentration of wealth and to impose limitations on private property in line with the public interest.

The Mexican Constitution created a representative, democratic, and federal system built upon universal suffrage. Nevertheless, it does not view democracy merely as a set of legal and political rules. Instead, democracy is seen as a pattern of life explicitly geared toward the overall improvement of the population and the economic and political defense of the nation.

The Mexican Constitution excluded religious groups from any kind of political activity in order to strengthen civil authority. Moreover, it set up a strong executive power. The presidential system, which is a common feature of the democracies in this hemisphere, took on sharper contours in Mexico due to our historical tradition and the need to harmonize political stability with social change. But the dangers of a concentration of power were checked by the principle of nonreelection, which favors a turnover in political leadership.

Despite the soundness of these principles, the years following the Revolution were agitated ones. The fundamental tasks to be accomplished were to create a modern administration and an infrastructure for material progress and to unite the country through education and better means of communication. To initiate such an ambitious program in a country ravaged by a decade of internal strife demanded skill, time, and energy. It was necessary to regulate the operation of political institutions and to further our social programs. But electoral disputes still gave rise to violent confrontations. In 1929, the death of President Obregón ended the period of the political bosses, the *caudillos*, and a crisis occurred that could only be solved by uniting the forces of the new regime within a single party: the Institutional Revolutionary Party (PRI).

The year 1979 marked the fiftieth year since the PRI was founded and since it began to govern. Its creation delineated two distinct eras in Mexican history: that of armed revolts and that of negotiated resolution of political conflicts. For this reason, it is a mistake to define the PRI as an exclusive power group. In order to capture its vitality, it is essential to see the PRI as a national coalition of political forces.

As the PRI gained power, Mexico was able to organize strong policies to counter the effects of the great depression that struck the world in the 1930s. Our country could not resort to conservative solutions; it had to take advantage of this opportunity to carry out the reforms that had been put off. Within a few years, most of the large landholdings had been divided up among the peasants. In addition, workers' organizations became noticeably stronger, and the recovery of our natural resources was begun as the foundation of an independent economic program. Thus the nationalization of the oil companies in 1938 marked the highest point of our revolution. Mexico came of age before the world by making sure that its sovereign rights would be respected, securing the basic principles of the Constitution from outside attack.

Unfortunately, the Second World War did not favor the continuation of profound social reforms. Mexico had to lessen internal tensions by encouraging national unity. At the same time, the country had to develop its agricultural economy to supply growing markets and embark on rapid development of its manufacturing in order to make industrialization possible. For several decades, our country attained high rates of economic growth, and rapid urbanization brought about an enlargement of the middle class and the industrial working class. The efforts made to attain the physical integration of the country, to provide it with water and electricity, and to meet the diverse demands of its population, are unquestionable. The statistics documenting our progress have been astonishing.

Political stability and fixed goals have enabled us to solve countless problems. Unfortunately, many others appeared with development. When the Revolution began, there were barely sixteen million Mexicans; now our population is nearing seventy million. Theoretically, the advances should have been sufficient to assure a considerable level of general well-being. However, things worked out quite differently: the changes that took place in Mexico brought about a population explosion, and although this in turn expedited growth our progress could not keep pace.

Whatever our population growth may be in the future, from now until the close of this century we shall have to build twice as much as we have previously. This is the main challenge to our political system, but it is not the only one. There are also serious doubts about the ability of our current economic models to satisfy our needs. Sharp inequality still prevails, and methods of development that are slow to spread prosperity have become glaringly inadequate. This social problem is our most serious national concern. To solve it calls for greater production, more extensive training and employment, and a much more just distribution of income. All of this must be done in an unfavorable international climate beset by inflation, the monetary crisis, trade protectionism, and lack of solidarity.

Today Mexico is preparing to face a crucial period, what President Lopez Portillo has called the "zero hour" of our history. Ours is a complex society that needs to maintain its political cohesion while it offers legitimate channels of expression to all. Our ongoing reforms seek to foster and strengthen a new national consensus about the goals and directions of the country.

We accept the risks of liberty. We wish to strengthen the state through, not against, democracy because an authoritarian system would lack sustenance and meaning. The essence of our political formula is still valid: continuity of principles, the ability to innovate and conciliate, and a social conscience in the exercise of power. Thus the ability of the Mexican state to guide development and safeguard national autonomy should not be taken lightly. Our political system has endured the most difficult trials; it has succeeded—at times in an exemplary fashion—in passing through the first stages of the modernization process.

Admittedly, we are on the threshold of particularly arduous times, but no more so than those that are in store for the great majority of developing countries. And we have an advantage: we have proven institutions, experience, national goals, and the prospect of abundant resources. Of other countries—and especially our neighbors—we only ask respect, understanding, and fair treatment. Mexico's problems are not the internal affair of any other nation; interdependence is not a weakening of our respective sovereignties. An understanding of this basic truth will do much to further an intelligent dialogue that truly involves the good will and sense of responsibility of both our countries.

Contradictions and Continuities in Mexican Constitutionalism

Fernando Pérez Correa

In 1972, in Ann Arbor, Michigan, over one thousand dissertations on Mexican topics written by North American graduate
students were catalogued. Their themes ranged from maritime
resources in the Gulf of Cortés to the geological formations of
the Mexican Caribbean. They also include, obviously, the history
and politics of Mexico. The Institutional Revolutionary Party
(PRI), the Mexican presidency, the cabinet, state and local governments, have all been the subjects of detailed histories that
compare favorably with works on Mexico written by Mexicans.
In addition, there are often conferences and meetings that
gather Mexicans and North Americans to discuss Mexican
topics. Indeed, the existing North American bibliography on
Mexico is mandatory for Mexican students. And this does not
include the enormous number of internal papers, diplomatic
exchanges, restricted circulation studies, and secret government
documents that are produced every year.

I believe it is significant that this symposium is called Mexico
Today rather than *Los Estados Unidos Hoy*. After all, I do not
recall any North American presidents having had Mexican
apologists, detractors, or prophets—as Mexican presidents have
found in the United States. Nor do I know of a Mexican book
about the United States with the pretentions of, say, Raymond

Vernon's book about nothing less than *The Dilemma of Mexico's Development*. It would seem, then, that our countries have been examined in rather different ways.

The cultural and social differences that underlie our development have made us different in our mode of understanding, different in the scope of our visions, different in our frame of reference, and different also in our definition of what can be manipulated and in our assessment of our capacity to manipulate. These perspectives, explicit or implicit, are not necessarily easy to grasp. I am not supposing that American authors unconsciously approach the analysis of Mexico in terms of its degree of Westernization, nor that they make it their purpose to show the conditions for such Westernization. I refer, rather, to the need for knowledge in order to judge and to the fact that when judging one inevitably employs one's own measure.

As part of a policy of progress fostered by the United States, the Mexican government may seem the very prototype of an instrument for the mobilization of social forces. On the other hand, the Mexican government may represent for the U.S. a regime of questionable viability and condemnable practices. In both cases, these judgments refer back to a North American model of democracy.

North American political scientists studying Mexico have engaged in research and analysis that is pervaded with their own ethos, which in turn has led to disagreement and contradiction. How does one account for a revolutionary regime that permits the deepening of social inequalities and the deterioration of those popular interests that sustain it? How does one explain the nature of a revolutionary regime that mobilizes social resources in order to generate the prosperity that strengthens privilege and property interests? This contradiction has elicited, naturally, hypotheses as far-fetched as that which pretends that Mexico suffers from a deep political schizophrenia. There are also those who maintain that there is no contradiction at all, that opposite interests meet in a deeper reality where rule and practice, values and actions, live in harmony.

Some authors (Robert E. Scott, for instance) have conceived of the Mexican system as a structure that integrates within the

Institutional Revolutionary Party interests whose capacity for conflict would be virtually limitless. Others think of the PRI as merely electoral machinery and of the system as an exploiting entity based on its capacity for manipulating social classes into a corporate scheme under the banner of the Revolution. Still others think of the system as being fundamentally pragmatic and geared to ad hoc measures, sensitive to conflict to the degree that the contending forces are important. In other words, some authors think of the system as one on the verge of collapse, others recommend more or less significant reforms, and still others believe that the system as it stands today is viable.

In my view, the nature of the Mexican system can be disassociated neither from its origins nor from the historical meaning of its political project. The Mexican Revolution was, among other things, a military movement that destroyed its opponents by force and established a strong government after a lengthy political crisis. The transfer of power was carried out by violent means in 1916, 1920, 1924, 1928, and 1929. The continuing theme of the Mexican presidential system is therefore that of a group defeating its opponents by force, the latter having also tried to gain power by force. Because of this, the President became the head of a social alliance whose military forces had been victorious. He became the center of a system of mediations between interests.

The strength of the Mexican president derives from his capacity to hold together a whole set of forces that are constantly changing. The social project of the 1920s has developed unevenly, sometimes fulfilling itself, sometimes not. Thus we need to see the goals of the Revolution as an essential element in the present interplay of forces. In other words, new social forces are admitted to the political realm to the degree that the Constitution is progressively applied.

Although there were cultural continuities and although attitudes to power remained the same, the Mexican regime changed after the Revolution. It transformed class relationships in the country as it suppressed serfdom, as it favored the strengthening of national forces over regional ones, and as it emphasized modernization. But this resulted in a major contradiction: the creation of structural and institutional conditions for development appeared alongside profound cultural and historical inequalities. Hence the system generated a national bourgeoisie as the instrument for modernization, but also set up the possibility that this group would try to define the course of modernization. For this reason, it was crucial for the Revolution to recruit and integrate those who had everything but money.

The creation of Mexico's great bourgeoisie also generated a crisis of legitimacy. In a revolutionary way, it shaped an opposition group against which the authoritarian style is at best uncomfortable. Nevertheless, various social forces were integrated into a national organization and achieved both representation and participation. There can be no doubt that in 1940, when the take-off of Mexico's capitalist society occurred, the forces that sustained the Revolution had achieved a fundamental participation in the world of politics through the PRI.

There is a further and more radical sense in which one can say that an understanding of the history of Mexico is essential to an understanding of the Mexican present. I am referring to the fact that Mexico's political leaders did not set up a new society but rather embarked on a project for the development of such a society. In other words, Mexican law is not perceived in a Hegelian manner, as the historical embodiment of the spirit of the nation. It is considered instead in a Kantian manner, as the progressive development of ideas in an endless march toward equality and democracy.

In 1917, Mexico was a rural, pre-industrial society; nevertheless, it had a Constitution that recognized collective bargaining powers, unions, the right to strike, and minimum wage conditions. That year the decisive confrontation between regional forces and national identity took place, and once again the state was confirmed as the power responsible for the irreversible shaping of the nation. The Constitution of 1917 confirmed the democratic and republican character of the state. Its federal and separate institutions were created from a system meant to govern indigenous minorities, a rural precapitalist world, in the midst of a revolution in which, among other things, it was possible that there could be a seizure of power by the enemies of democracy. In the face of this, the Constitution reaffirmed the will of the state to establish the individual's rights, although the shaping of citizens was still largely a project for the future. The idea of this project was to build a nation endowed with the capacity to define its destiny and to mobilize its internal forces. In other words, Mexico was starting from a pre-industrial, pre-liberal and predemocratic society and imbuing it with democratic values, Christian humanism, egalitarianism, and, above all, the will to progress.

I have said that the Revolution was made up of a constellation of forces that sustained the development and consolidation of a new state. At the creation of this state in 1917, the political class was recruited from the remnants of the old leading classes—the elites—but also from craftsmen, representatives of good Christian families, intellectuals born under the old regime, new types of farmers, and other local figures of the new order. This political class was charged with the responsibility not only for the workings of the state machinery, but also for the progress of national integration and the achievement of the revolutionary goals. However, this political class was neither homogeneous nor loyal to a homogeneous, theoretical body. In this context, for example, the agrarian reform can be seen as a desire to return to the notion of the self-sufficient family within the community. But it also encompassed a project for the development of a cattle-farming society and even a proposal for the development of a capitalist-oriented, organized agriculture.

A similar complexity can be seen in the radicalism of the workers, which stressed nationalist rights against foreign enterprise. At the same time, however, national interests were to have priority over the rights of workers in the public sector. Development was to be given priority over working class egoism.

Once again, however, the capacity to make use of new opportunities was unequally distributed, and those sectors of the population that had already pushed into modernization developed to the detriment of those sectors that were, in fact, the support of the new national society. The rates of prosperity in the modern sector, combined with the process of stagnation in the marginalized world, generated major inequalities. These inequalities also meant that certain interests were not adequately defended. Thus it might be said that while the state emphasized the need for economic growth as a prerequisite for an improvement in the quality of life, at the same time it gave private enterprise the power to determine the ways and the rate of growth to be achieved. This transferred from the state to private enterprise a certain legitimacy—and therefore limited the state's own viability.

The private sector occupies a key place in the development process, and it has made the state feel the real weight of its importance. Indeed, the Echeverría administration may have shown that the state is no longer in a position to renegotiate the limits to which its own historical role has been reduced. However, the private sector had, in 1976, what the popular forces had in 1968: a suspension of the routine practices of the system and an extraordinary moment when anything seemed possible. But the private sector failed to produce an organization determined to acquire power; it failed to define the balance of social interest to be preserved.

In this light, the present Mexican regime can be seen as a pragmatic one that is sensitive to the specific weight of conflicting forces, aware that the fundamental crisis of the system always occurs when the state's enemies refuse to negotiate. Sonnenfelt maintains that the basis, the very essence of the Mexican system, is precisely its capacity to adjust conflicting interests: the notion of political bargaining power presupposes the existence of a political style in which coexistence is preferable to the suppression of one of society's components. Small gains are of greater importance than a game in which one player gains everything or nothing; tactical advances or retreats become strategic victories. Thus the present political reform is a concrete form of bargaining between the government and its opponents. The present use of workers' demands is a specific form of bargaining. Refusal to negotiate is the ultimate sign of rejection of the social contract, evidence of a return to confrontational politics of the sort that would eventually redefine the social pact.

For the Mexican leftist parties this fact is particularly significant. Today they feel they must negotiate with the state because they are aware that the only short-run alternative to the present form of government would be a military regime. For the left, the government is distinguishable from the state, but within the state are forces of the left that the government is unable to integrate or represent. This is perhaps one of the major contradictions of the current political reform—recognizing institutionally as a basis of legitimacy not the demands of the old revolutionary left, but the electoral will of the central majority, the new bourgeoisie of the private sector.

For the left, the current political reform means that in Mexico there exists a real tradition of struggle, that social progress has generated new forces not only for the privileged, but also on behalf of equality, and that politics is concerned not so much with imagination as with organization. Politics, in Mexico as elsewhere, does not concern the desirable but the possible.

Elites, Masses, and Parties

Rafael Segovia

Describing the nations that achieved independence after the Second World War, the French sociologist and philosopher Raymond Aron wrote: "In many of those cases, the state came to existence before the nation. There was nationalism in search of nations." If we look to the historical development of Mexico, we must see the truth in Aron's words.

In Mexico, a small and tightly knit group first implemented the ideals of nationhood and freedom. But in the general population, the desire for independence was not widespread, at least in part because of the dependent colonial situation in which the vast majority of the population, divided into social classes and castes, lacked political rights. Nevertheless, some of the Creoles (the descendants of the Spaniards), men who were able to get good jobs, men who went through schools or colleges and even studied in the university, were thinking in terms different from those fostered by the Spanish crown. Some of these priests, miners, tradesmen, landowners, and soldiers were in favor of the creation of a new nation. And in 1821 they got it.

In that year, Mexico was an independent nation, and in some ways a new nation. But the social structure did not change overnight. Castes and slavery were abolished, but not poverty, illness, and illiteracy. Social and political inequality remained. The real change came with the new project that was created by the demand for independence, as it was reflected in our constitutional history, where we can trace the influence of the European Enlightenment, the United States Constitution, and the Spanish liberal tradition, all of which demanded greater participation by the common people. But if nonegalitarian social bases were rejected by North Americans and Europeans, the core of the problem for Mexico remained the political rights of the common people, which were very frequently limited in one way or another.

It was a small, elite group of Mexicans that insisted on the inclusion of a much more sizable part of the population in the political game—but at the same time, they knew that the very existence of Mexico as a nation demanded as strong a state as possible. Thus the social problem, and its possible solution, produced a disruptive situation that jeopardized not only society but the new nation itself. In Mexico the individual can be restrained only by the state—not by the collective free will of the people. For this reason, social inequality was and remains too great; in consequence, it was, and is, impossible to have social groups check and balance one another.

In 1917, the new Constitution enhanced the role of the state as the most important player in the political arena, and its legitimacy was founded in a new national project that we could call modernization. Modernization asked inevitably for participation, but to what extent would full and unrestrained participation endanger the modernizing project? Participation, in Mexico as in any other part of the world, has two faces—the individual and the state (I consider the state to be something different from the simple sum total of the personal will of each single citizen). Therefore, the openness of the state to the pressure of political groups and individuals was and remains a delicate matter. Gradually, then, diversification and specialization of industrial, intellectual, worker, and peasant groups, among others, brought changes in political organization until today we have not only new political parties, but also a very sophisticated system of pressure groups and lobbies.

From both tradition and necessity, the revolutionary government strove to include in the ranks of its organization all the relevant forces in Mexican society. From 1921 on, the National

Revolutionary Party (PNR), known as the grandfather of the present-day PRI, enlarged its affiliation and to some extent identified itself with the nation—with all the Mexicans who accepted the principles of the Revolution. But the modernization process that the state was implementing created ever more sophisticated specialization within the country's social groups. These changes were reflected by the PRI reforms enacted in 1932 and 1937. Moreover, in 1939, the creation of the National Action Party recognized the existence of a center-right coalition in Mexican politics.

In the 1940s, as a result of the Second World War, a new policy of national union was established by the government and a new kind of legitimacy was developed. Although the revolutionary legitimacy—that is to say, the national project of modernization—was maintained and sustained, a new dimension was added in the form of electoral legitimization. The government knew that some form of dissent was unavoidable and that the best way to channel this dissent was through electoral politics. However, this process also presented the danger of factionalization and an extreme regionalization of public opinion. After all, the situation that existed in the 1920s, when more than 3,000 separate party groups supported the candidacy of Obregón, would be disastrous in a modernizing country.

For this reason, the electoral law of 1946 was a demanding one. The conditions imposed by the government for the participation of political parties in the national elections were almost impossible to fulfill, and only three organizations managed to present candidates. Not surprisingly, the opposition parties won only a few representatives in the lower chamber and none in the upper chamber—until 1963, when the Constitution was reformed and the opposition went to parliament through party deputies (a special kind of election). This law has been criticized on many occasions, but it must be understood as another implementation of the political philosophy of the revolutionary government. In accepting the opposition party's participation as far as that opposition represents a sizable segment of public opinion and shows a clear capacity for organization, the state is shaping a new political system wider than the one that was created in 1929 with the formation of the Institutional Revolutionary Party, the PRI.

There is also immense bargaining power within the Mexican political system, as seen in the public discussions of the new electoral law, which specifies electoral procedures and the rights and duties of political parties, monitors the political utilization of the mass media, and regulates the form of electoral participation established by the Constitution of 1917. The impetus for this law came from the fact that in the last twenty years the demand for more popular participation has grown at a faster rate than during the whole of the nineteenth century, creating a tense situation among the parties. In order to avoid a clash, as happened in 1968, the Constitution and the electoral law were amended in 1973 and again in 1977. These modifications brought an increasing number of opposition representatives to the Chamber of Deputies, and in the largest cities of the country the opposition parties made gains they had never thought possible.

In 1973, when the PRI carried the Federal District (Mexico City) by a bare 51 percent, a new kind of balance was achieved. The elections of 1975, however, proved disastrous for the opposition, both left and right. The Popular Socialist Party and the National Action Party split into several factions. It was impossible to achieve agreement in the ranks, and the opposition accordingly lost a significant number of electoral districts. No one challenged the presidential candidacy of José López Portillo.

If 1975 was a disastrous year for the opposition, it was also a disastrous year for the PRI. Today the majority party needs the presence of political resistance. The democratic credibility of the country depends on a real political contest. Thus in 1976 an agreement was made with a new opposition party. The bargaining position of the government was a delicate one, and the rejection by some groups of an unexpected and rather dangerous situation, the legalization of the Communist Party, was viewed with some concern. Nevertheless, after a protracted and difficult negotiation, a new electoral law was adopted in 1978, and some surprises were predicted in the 1979 balloting. Even if the PRI had suffered severe losses, its members, in common with all voters, could be expected to benefit from a new and broader Mexican democracy.

In this context, we should remember the words of Moyo Palencio, Mexico's former Home Secretary: "A vote against the PRI is a vote for the system." The state has not resigned its role in Mexico. It is still, after fifty years of PRI rule, the most important organizational factor in the country. The modernizing process in Mexico began in 1929, and we must realize that modernization, participation, individual rights, and opposition are all inextricably linked.

ESSAY 7

Urban Development in Mexico

Luis Unikel

Since 1940, Mexico has experienced one of the most rapid and lasting processes of socioeconomic development in the Third World. As a result, Mexico has also experienced intense urban development, producing a massive concentration of population in existing or emerging cities.

In 1940, Mexico was predominantly a rural nation: 72.4 percent of its population lived in communities of fewer than 5,000 inhabitants, dependent upon an agricultural economy. Currently, a little more than half the population lives in urban communities and is part of an urban economy. During the first half of this century, the urban population almost tripled, to 3.9 million people. By 1970, 22 million people lived in cities, a fivefold increase in only twenty years. At present, Mexico's urban population is estimated at 34 million people.

While the urban population has been soaring, the rural population has continued to show a slow but steady growth, despite the influx from the rural areas to the urban centers. Thus the rural population increased from 14 million in 1940 to 23 million in 1970. By 1979, it was estimated at 27 million.

If we examine urban population growth more closely, we find that during the decade from 1940 to 1950 the net migration to the cities accounted for 59 percent of their total growth. The country's natural population growth continued to increase as well, and during the following two decades (1950–1970), this

71

natural growth exercised a relatively greater weight than the rural-urban migration (up to 68 percent during the period from 1960 to 1970). Today, however, the birth rate is declining, and, as the 1980 census figures show, the natural growth of the urban population and the net migration from the countryside have about the same proportional weight in the total growth of Mexico's urban centers.

In 1940 we also saw the first signs that urbanized areas in Mexico were being formed through the integration of nearby nonurban communities with major cities. The Mexico City region was one of the first and most conspicuous examples of this phenomenon, but today the same trend can be found in many medium-sized cities, such as Cuernavaca and Tampico. However, the cities on the northern border, some of which have shown the most rapid demographic growth in the country, should be seen as rather special cases. Their expansion must be considered along with that experienced by neighboring North American cities: together they form international urbanized areas that have socioeconomic and political importance for both countries. A particularly noteworthy example, with a population of close to a million, is the urban area of Ciudad Juárez-El Paso.

These patterns in the distribution of the population reveal two opposing tendencies: a relatively high percentage of Mexico's people crowds into the main urban centers, while the remnant lives in tens of thousands of sparsely populated localities dispersed throughout the provinces. While urban development has reached more and more regions of the country, these are mainly the areas that are more advanced economically. There were 55 urban centers in 1940, 178 in 1970, and over 200 by 1980. More impressive is the fact that by 1970 the number of cities with 100,000 or more inhabitants was almost six times that of 1940.

While it is true that Mexico's population is becoming more and more concentrated, and that the rural areas are slowly being depleted, it is important to remember that in absolute terms the rural population is still increasing. The number of people living in communities of less than a thousand inhabitants increased from 9.8 million in 1940 to 13.5 million by the beginning of

1970 (approximately 28 percent of the national population). The present figure is a smaller percentage, but it is still growing and is now about 15 million people. Naturally, the incorporation of this segment of the population into the economic and social development of the country is difficult since this group remains marginal. The poor conditions prevailing in such small communities convert this part of Mexico's population into a potential source of migrants.

In contrast to the scattered smaller communities, the bulk of Mexico's urban population is found in only a few areas. The most important of these is Mexico City, which accounted for 17 percent of the total population in 1970 and about 20 percent eight years later. Even more significant, however, is the fact that this population is responsible for about half of the country's economic production. This highlights another feature of Mexico's population distribution, its regional imbalance. Out of the nation's 32 states, 14 can be considered the most developed: 8 are in the north, while 3 others are around Mexico City and Guadalajara. In contrast, almost all of the poorest states are in the south.

For the next twenty years, Mexico's urban population growth will depend on the pattern followed by its natural increase, assuming that net urban migration maintains its present growth rate. If the total population reaches between 100 and 109 million people (a recent low estimate established by the National Population Council), Mexico would then have from 68 to 74 million people concentrated in urban centers of 15,000 or more inhabitants, and it would be possible to expect the Mexico City Metropolitan Area (MCMA) to have between 21 and 24 million people. If, however, this estimate does not hold true or if migration to Mexico City continues at the same rate as it does today, it is possible that the Metropolitan Area will not be far from the 30 million mark, as part of a total urban population of 80 to 85 million people.

For obvious reasons, Mexico's urban concentration and regional imbalance have stirred vehement arguments about the country's economic development and aroused the serious concern of the government. Measures to foster regional de-

velopment outside the Mexico City region have been implemented since the 1940s, and some have been quite successful—
the Irrigation and River Basin Programs, for example, whose
first River Basin Commission was a replica of the Tennessee
Valley Authority. Nevertheless, industrialization policies since
the 1940s have largely contributed to the present excessive concentration of socioeconomic activities and population in the
MCMA by giving preferential treatment to the metropolis, not
only indirectly (in the construction or extension of communications and transportation systems, power and water supplies, and
such facilities as hospitals, schools, and institutions of higher
learning), but also directly (through fiscal incentives and protective tariffs and subsidies to industrial firms locating first in the
Federal District and later in its contiguous metropolitan area in
the State of Mexico).

Since 1970, however, under mounting pressure to act in
dealing with the MCMA's growing concentration of population
and economic and cultural activities, the federal government has
shown greater concern for both sectoral and territorial development. This interest led to a rush of legislative activity: a
plethora of laws, agreements, presidential decrees, trust companies, and fiscal and promotional instruments that were en-
gineered to limit the establishment of industry in the MCMA
and foster regional development. The ultimate goal of the economic policy was to carry through both economic expansion and
income redistribution. This new approach to the problem of
regional development was prompted by the Echeverría administration's great concern about the acute regional disparities and
by the president's determination to remedy the situation
through the promotion of regional development programs and
industrial decentralization.

The programs developed during this period included fiscal
incentives to industries to locate outside the three largest urban
centers (1971–1972 legislation); the construction and promotion
of industrial parks, cities, and complexes, as well as commercial
centers in a large number of cities (through trust funds, since
December 1970); the establishment of trust funds in every state
to identify and promote small and medium-sized industries

(since June 1971); the provision of credit and other forms of assistance to small and medium-sized industries; and the generation of employment through the "twin plant" industries (initially confined to the northern border cities, this program was extended to the nation in October 1973). The most important development measure taken by the end of the Echeverría administration was the promulgation of the Law of Human Settlements, which called for a national urban development plan, state and municipal urban development plans, and plans for particular urban areas. This was the point of departure from which the present government created a new Ministry of Human Settlement and Public Works, as well as a National Urban Development Commission.

In complying with the Human Settlements Law, the Commission formulated a National Urban Development Plan in 1977 that became law in May 1978. This plan aims to reduce Mexico's urban concentration and its regional disparities by drastically limiting the growth of the Mexico City Metropolitan Area and not allowing it to go over 20 million people by the year 2000; by controlling the growth of the next two major cities, Monterrey and Guadalajara, to within 3 to 5 million people each; by fostering or controlling the growth of 11 middle-sized cities to a million people; and by encouraging 74 other smaller cities to grow to between 100,000 and 500,000 inhabitants. (One of the important middle-sized priority areas in the plan is Coatzacoalcos-Minatitlan on the Gulf Coast, Mexico's major oil complex.) All this is based on the hypothesis that the total population of the country will reach only 104 million people by the end of the century, which assumes a 10 percent population growth by the year 2000.

What are the chances of achieving the goals of the National Urban Development Plan? In my opinion, the prospects do not look good. In the first place, in order to slow down population growth in the Mexico City Metropolitan Area to any significant extent, it is essential to apply a series of measures for socioeconomic development in those regions with greater medium- and long-term growth possibilities. But these must be coupled with others that will discourage economic growth in the MCMA. The latter, obviously unpopular, would in the short run negatively affect the national economy since approximately half of the country's production is concentrated in the MCMA. Decreased public investment in the Mexico City area would also cause unemployment and would primarily affect the population with lower incomes, lessening their chances of getting running water, sewage, schools, parks, and employment. Obviously, such a plan would be very unpopular and could increase social tension.

This is one of the many dilemmas that any radical policy would provoke. One possible alternative would be to establish a strategy of regional development geared toward improving socioeconomic conditions in selected areas of the provinces, both urban and rural. Once the first positive results of this program are attained, it would be possible to put into practice selective discouragement measures to reduce the long-term rate of growth in the MCMA. Within the MCMA, however, it appears that the same problems are bound to persist to a greater or lesser extent. Similarly, for the governments of the Federal District and the State of Mexico, there seems to be no alternative other than to improve what has been done so far and to continue what can be defined as the art of the possible.

Economic and Social Development in Mexico

Victor L. Urquidi

Over the past forty years, Mexico has been moderately success-ful in achieving economic growth but relatively unsuccessful in bringing about an integrated and balanced process of social de-velopment. In 1938, when the foreign petroleum companies were expropriated, the economy was on the decline. Mexico had barely recovered from the ravages of the revolution that had ended in 1921. During the twenties, some modest institution-building had taken place, some highways and dams had been built, and some encouragement had been given to agriculture and industry. But the output of petroleum, the country's main export, had fallen throughout the period as oil discoveries in Venezuela were brought into production by the same companies that were reducing their Mexican investments, alarmed by the new nationalism that prevailed there. After 1929, the world de-pression also left its mark on Mexican mining. Thus the thirties were a period of stagnation, financial difficulty, and general unemployment. Migrants who had ventured across the northern border were driven back by the North American depression and swelled the ranks of the unemployed.

However, Mexico at that time was a predominantly agricul-tural country, and most people survived on very little in the rural areas. When the nationalization of the oil industry came

77

about, it was symbolic of the dawn of a new era, one in which the nation would embark on its own development pattern and cease to be merely a supplier of raw materials and an importer of manufactured consumer goods.

Today, forty years later, the Mexican economy can be characterized as semi-industrial. Thirty percent of its labor force is in manufacturing, construction, and transportation; another 30 percent is in trade and services; and only 40 percent is in agriculture. Since the 1940s, when Mexico's total steel output capacity was only 180,000 tons and its overall electric power generating capacity a mere 680,000 kw, a vast transformation has taken place.

During the forties, policies favoring industrialization, aided by the impact of World War II, helped expand Mexico's industrial base, carried out important state enterprise projects, and encouraged both domestic and foreign private investment. In the ensuing three decades, industrial growth was spectacular, supported by energy development, by the incorporation of new technologies, by improvements in the educational system and in labor training, and by appropriate financial policies. Today, Mexico's steel output capacity is over 5 million tons, and its electricity generation capacity is more than 12 million kilowatts. It is also significant that crude petroleum output, which hit a low of 35 million barrels per year in the early forties, had risen to an annual rate of over 400 million barrels in mid-1978. Meanwhile, production of refined petroleum products, which accounted for a mere 33 million barrels in 1938, was close to 300 million in 1978.

During this long period, a vast array of petrochemicals has been developed. In addition, metalworking, pulp and paper, chemicals and pharmaceuticals, domestic appliances, automobiles and trucks, agricultural machinery, electrical equipment, and a host of other intermediate and consumer goods industries have expanded in response to the domestic market and to new export demand. Traditional industries such as food and textiles, which employ a large percentage of the industrial labor force, have also increased their production. A modest development has been achieved as well in the capital goods sector. Over the past forty years, Mexico's overall industrial output has increased at an average of 7 to 8 percent annually—in other words, it doubles every 9 to 10 years.

Despite the emphasis on industrial development during this period, the agricultural sphere has not been neglected. With the opening of irrigation districts in the forties and fifties, Mexico was able to become self-sufficient in wheat, and eventually even an exporter. Many other cash crops were developed for both the domestic and foreign (mainly United States) markets. Production of corn, the staple item in the Mexican diet, increased with the cultivation of new lands and the introduction of improved seeds. High-yielding varieties of wheat were also developed. In fact, it can be said that the "Green Revolution" started in Mexico in the 1950s.

A large number of other crops signaled Mexico's agricultural boom, including cotton, coffee, sugar cane, and oil seeds, among others. Indeed, until the middle sixties, Mexican agricultural output, including livestock and fisheries, increased at an annual rate of approximately 4 percent, a rate surpassed by very few countries. Unfortunately, this rate began slowing down considerably in the late 1960s.

Thus, once we have stated its achievements, we must also acknowledge that Mexico's impressive growth record must be qualified. Its industrial expansion took place under a highly protective system, patterned on a nondirected import substitution process. A largely captive domestic market disguised the fact that much of the manufacturing industry lacked cost-effectiveness and could not compete in international markets. Moreover, production was concentrated in large enterprises, many of them subsidiaries of multinational corporations, at the expense of small and medium-sized businesses. In addition, the introduction of labor-saving technology contributed to a slower growth of industrial employment than might have been expected. Furthermore, as time went on, many gaps developed in the industrial structure, and dependence on imported intermediate products became larger than it had been before. The manufacture of capital goods lagged far behind the needs of the domestic market. To some extent, financial constraints prevented the timely expansion of Mexico's industrial capacity.

In agriculture, the imbalances were even more acute because modernization took place mostly on irrigated lands, for the benefit of a relatively small number of farmers, and with limited effects on employment. The bulk of rural Mexico, consisting of rain-fed and semi-arid lands, produced a declining share of the total agricultural output, with hardly any increase in average yields. This resulted in the continued maintenance of vast numbers of low-income peasant holdings that allowed only a meager standard of living and very limited access to finance, and that faced every sort of handicap in food production and marketing.

As this unbalanced structure developed within both the industrial and the agricultural sectors, the overall picture was affected by far-reaching demographic changes, both in numbers of people and in their geographic distribution. In 1940, Mexico was a country of 20 million inhabitants with a birth rate of close to 45 per thousand and a death rate of 22 per thousand, producing a growth rate of 2.3 percent per year. With the decline of mortality as a result of health programs and the progress of medicine, the growth rate had accelerated to nearly 3.5 percent annually by 1970. Mortality had fallen to 9 per thousand, while the birth rate remained in the neighborhood of 43 per thousand. With an estimated 50.4 million inhabitants in 1970, Mexico had become one of the fastest-growing nations in the world, with a doubling time of 20 years and a built-in potential for rapid population growth for decades to come, since 46 percent of the population was below the age of fifteen. In 1970, every Mexican woman of childbearing age was being replaced by 2.7 females likely to reach that function. (By way of comparison, in the United States this ratio is on the order of one to one, or slightly less.) Although the Mexican birth rate began to decline in 1973, largely as a result of family planning programs, and although targets for lower growth rates have been set for the rest of the century, today's 67 million Mexicans will inevitably surge past the 100 million mark by the year 2000, and to higher levels well into the next century.

Mexico's rapid population growth has been accompanied by an intense process of migration from rural areas to the major cities. Of course, this sort of migration is a normal feature of any developing country, but in Mexico, as in other Latin American nations, rural poverty has undoubtedly speeded up the process. Unfortunately, industrial and service development has not created enough jobs to employ the migrants in regular salaried work.

While income differentials between urban and rural employment play a key role in internal migration, there are also cultural and social factors that lead the younger generations to move off the farms. The rate at which this process has occurred in Mexico has resulted in large part in the creation of a vast army of underemployed and unemployed in the urban areas. The metropolitan area of Mexico City, with a population of over 13 million people, probably has 4 million persons in marginal occupations living in substandard conditions. Similar scenarios, albeit on a smaller scale, can be found in most major cities in Mexico. This includes the towns along the border, which operate as a staging ground for migration to the North American side, largely in response to the demand in the southern and western states for unskilled and low-wage labor in farming and service occupations.

Thus the structural imbalance in the Mexican economy, the high rate of growth of the population, and the intensive migration from the rural areas have contributed to a high rate of unemployment, which is now estimated at over 8 percent of the labor force. To this must be added a rate of underemployment of not less than 25 percent. This means that over 3 million available person-years are not utilized in Mexico in any economic activity. This figure would be even larger if the participation rate of women in the labor force were higher. Approximately 800,000 new jobs must be created each year merely to absorb the additions to the labor force that are derived from population growth, without taking into account already existing numbers of unemployed and underemployed. This gives some idea of the magnitude and nature of Mexico's development problem and illustrates the need for a new strategy in the next two decades.

With a per capita income of close to $1,000, Mexico can be classified among the advanced developing nations. Nevertheless, the patterns of development followed over the past forty years have failed to make any significant change in the distribution of personal income. According to recent surveys, the top 10 percent of income-earners appropriates about 40 percent of the country's total income, while the lower 40 percent receives barely 10 percent. Although there has probably been some improvement in the middle-income ranges, it can still be said that Mexico has one of the worst income distributions of any developing country. Inequality between the highest and lowest income levels is in the range of 35 or even 40 to 1.

The explanation for this gap is to be found not only in the difference between modern and traditional agriculture, or between modern high-technology industry and services and small-scale enterprise, or between self-employment and underemployment. It also has to do with the kind of society that has developed in the course of three centuries of Spanish colonial rule and a hundred years of post-Independence liberal, capitalistic economic evolution, as well as with the ambiguous mixed-economy regime that arose from the 1917 Constitution.

Mexico's revolutionary Constitution of 1917 provides for free enterprise, but it gives a strong social direction and content to the state, which takes responsibility for the development of education, land reform, the rights of labor, natural resources, and, where appropriate, any other economic and social activity. Acting on the Constitution and the many laws deriving from it, the Mexican state has undertaken vast programs in education, health, and medical care; in the protection of indigenous peoples and children; in improving wages and working conditions. It has also carried out land reform to the extent that a substantial part of the land is now in peasant holdings and small and medium-sized private properties (although there are still 3 to 4 million landless peasants). It has nationalized oil and gas resources and expropriated the foreign companies. It has regulated farm prices and markets. It has established public enterprises in many branches of industry, in transportation and communications, in trade, and in financial and other services. It has nationalized electricity generation and distribution. And it exerts a strong influence, through regulation and financial and trade policy, on private investment (including foreign investment) in almost every field. Nevertheless, the command of the state over financial resources, through taxation as well as through borrowing and pricing policies, has not been sufficient to enable it to develop fully an economic structure that would guarantee high employment levels and meet the essential needs of the country and its people.

Within the mixed economy framework, and within its regulations, every sort of incentive has been given to private enterprise, both domestic and foreign, to expand industry, agriculture, trade, and services. The private sector, by and large, has followed its perceived market orientations and, to a large extent, has invested in consumer goods for the rising middle class, as well as in certain intermediate agricultural and industrial products. Given great protection, it has concentrated on the domestic market and has paid little attention to export markets. It has introduced mainly labor-saving technology, without consideration for local conditions. It has carried out very little industrial research, which in turn has led to a costly dependence on foreign technology. It has neglected the production of simple, basic products for the vast low-income groups. It has distributed high profits to a very concentrated ownership and has failed to reinvest sufficiently, relying too heavily on borrowing from domestic and foreign banks. It has resisted tax reform, both personal and corporate, to such an extent that Mexico has one of the lowest overall tax burdens among developing countries.

I do not mean to downgrade the achievements of domestic and foreign private enterprise in Mexican economic development, nor to minimize the important role played by state enterprise and policies. However, it is a matter of record that the patterns of Mexican economic growth have so far failed to produce a system that may assure Mexico's rapidly increasing population an equitable distribution of benefits, even when the expanding social and educational programs are taken into account.

It is fair to add that the Mexican economy, dependent as it is upon the world economy, has had considerable difficulties with the trade policies of the industrially advanced nations and with their specific import restrictions. The recent recession and stagflation in these countries also have served to limit Mexican exports. On the other hand, in the last twenty years, and even more so in recent times, Mexico has enjoyed fairly easy access to long-term international loans and to short- and medium-term financing from foreign banking systems. Nevertheless, the condition of Mexican economic and social development is the result of the particular view and strategy worked out by Mexico itself, under the particular political circumstances of the past forty years, and under both internal and external pressures.

The years from 1975 to 1978 were years of deep financial and economic crisis, compounded by the effects of the devaluation of the peso in August of 1976. The economy slowed down considerably and unemployment increased. Inflation stood at 46 percent in 1976, at 20 percent in 1977, and above 16 percent in 1978. Gradually, the outlook has improved, and there are indications that industrial production and construction are picking up. One of the most significant developments is linked to the growth in oil and gas production in the mid-70s, which not only helped a great deal in tiding over the financial and monetary crisis, but held out a radically changed prospect for Mexico's future.

By 1972, despite considerable investments in petroleum exploration and production, Mexico had become a net importer of crude oil. At about that time, extraordinarily important new oilfields were discovered in the southeast, both on land and offshore. These were to lead to Mexico's virtual self-sufficiency in oil production by 1974 and to an export surplus of 34 million barrels in 1975. By 1977, exports had risen to 74 million barrels, and nearly doubled in 1978. International prices were such that 1978 gross exports of crude petroleum amounted to approximately $2 billion, making petroleum Mexico's principal export, as important to the national economy as tourist revenue. Although imports of equipment by the oil industry absorbed a considerable share of this gross income, as exports of both crude and refined oil increased they were correctly estimated to reach over $5 billion by 1980 (an amount that does not include petrochemicals and gas). In mid-1978, oil and gas reserves were estimated to be on the order of 20 billion barrels of proven reserves, with a probability of 30 billion and a potential of 200 billion.

Thus Mexico became almost overnight a petroleum supplier of the first magnitude, both in potential for the rest of the century and in actual output. By 1982, Mexico plans to reach a production of 2.2 million barrels per day, which will allow an export surplus of 1.1 million barrels daily. The obvious question arises: quite apart from Mexico's potential role as a supplier of oil and gas to an energy-hungry world, how will this sudden wealth and revenue affect Mexico's development prospects? And, more precisely, will the removal of financial constraints help solve Mexico's fundamental structural problems in the economic and social spheres?

It should be pointed out that this is not the first time in history that the Mexican economy has had a boom in its export sector. One need only recall the silver boom of the sixteenth century, as well as the mining booms that occurred in the late eighteenth century and once again toward the end of the nineteenth century. Mexico experienced a significant oil boom during the 1920s, and there was a not inconsiderable foreign trade surplus during World War II. However, there are two factors that distinguish the current oil boom. First, since the oil industry is nationalized, the surplus foreign exchange and fiscal revenue will accrue to the state, and second, Mexico has reached a critical stage in its development process. The population explosion and the extreme inequalities produced in the past forty years have created a situation that is without precedent, a situation in which the state can allocate vast additional resources and set out a pattern of development that not only may meet the basic needs of the population, but also may create new agricultural and industrial wealth and provide rapidly rising employment levels.

Of course, the basic needs of Mexico's people are great. Twenty million Mexicans still live in communities of less than a thousand people, most without proper water supply and drainage, without modern communications, and with minimum agricultural productivity. A further 8 to 10 million persons live in marginal urban areas, without proper housing, water, or drainage. There are some 8 million illiterates over the age of seven, and another 20 million who are functional illiterates. Over one half of the labor force has had less than three years of schooling (in the manufacturing industry, this figure is about 35 percent). Less than 4 percent of the gross national product is spent on education. There is a housing deficit in urban areas of some 3 million units. Infant mortality is still on the order of 60 per thousand children born. Close to 30 percent of the population is undernourished. In other words, a very large segment of Mexico's population is in a state of poverty that is socially unacceptable and that cannot be conducive to a stable and progressive society.

There is a general awareness that the petroleum revenues present a unique opportunity to channel resources in order to bring about a more balanced economic structure and to provide for future alternative sources of industrial and agricultural wealth, as well as for other sources of energy. The Mexican government has announced that a special development fund will be constituted from its oil revenues, but it remains to be seen just how this fund will operate and what its principles and policies will be. In Mexico's fairly open society, it can be expected that waste and inefficiency will inevitably be a part of the new stage of development. But it can also be hoped that some good use will be made of the oil revenues.

Success in dealing with the employment problem, both current and prospective, remains the crucial test of Mexico's development strategy for the rest of this century. The demographic component of the problem will tend to diminish as the birth rate continues to fall, especially after an interval of twelve to fifteen years. But the demand for labor within Mexico that results from the country's development strategy will be the key to the sort of social structure that may be expected in the future, and to the stability of the system as a whole.

PART 3

MEXICO AND THE WORLD

Mexico: Viewpoints of a Country of Intermediate Development on the World Economy

Bernardo Sepúlveda Amor

Mexico shares the problems and aspirations of all developing nations. However, as a country of intermediate development, Mexico is facing the particular problems of a semi-industrialized nation on the way toward more advanced stages of its economic evolution.

Economically speaking, Mexico initiated its "breakthrough" during the Second World War, and was able to achieve a degree of industrialization through a policy of import substitution, particularly in consumer goods and certain intermediate products. The development model that was used for the next thirty years generated a 7 percent growth in real terms throughout this entire period, a feat unequalled by any other developing country. Success was also achieved in stabilizing prices, so that during the last ten years of this model—from 1960 to 1970—prices rose by an annual rate of 5 percent.

In order to explain the scope of Mexico's modernization process it might be useful to consider a few statistics. Mexico is the thirteenth largest country in the world in land area, the tenth in population, and the fourteenth in gross domestic production; it is among the world's twenty leading producers of steel, energy, lead, sulfuric acid, cement, and automobiles; and it is among the five top producers of silver, sulfur, zinc, fluorite, mercury, and antimony. On the basis of any of the eight criteria established by the United Nations, Mexico is among the nineteen leading countries of the world in terms of standards of living.

Nevertheless, there are great problems that Mexico has not been able to resolve. Some of these have become even more serious—for example, the concentration of income in certain sectors of the population and in certain regions of the country. Forty percent of Mexico's population lives in rural areas and lives off the land. Nevertheless, this sector accounts for a mere 11 percent of the gross domestic product, whereas the services sector, which does not contribute any real added value to the economy, accounts for 35 percent of the gross domestic product. In addition, Mexico continues to be a country with serious deficiencies in food, education, housing, and health.

Clearly, Mexico's needs are both varied and multifaceted. We require technology, capital, and access to the markets of the developed countries, just as other developing countries do. However, our needs are also a reflection of our intermediate stage of development. In this difficult transitional period, any attempt by Mexico to accept all the economic obligations and rules instituted by the developed countries and to compete with them on equal trade bases in all areas would be not only inequitable, but also hardly viable. In fact, such a course of action would slow down the country's development and prevent it from achieving the goals it has set for itself.

Mexico's needs have been principally satisfied with its internal resources. However, as in the case of a large number of nonindustrialized countries, domestic savings cannot finance the huge investment required by an accelerated development process. Although it would be possible for the developing countries to attain investment levels that would not overreach their domestic savings levels, this would result in very low growth rates and would only intensify already existing problems. For this reason, Mexico must have access to sources abroad through loans and/or foreign investment. To pay its debts, Mexico must obtain foreign exchange, and such exchange is received from foreign trade.

In the last thirty years, world trade has grown at an annual average rate of 7.1 percent. However, this average is the result of a 7.5 percent growth rate by the developed countries and a growth rate of only 5.9 percent for the developing countries. This disparity can be partially explained by the fact that exports of primary agricultural products, to which the developing countries contribute a high proportion in world trade, increased by only 2.6 percent yearly. It is also important to note that approximately 40 percent of the increase in real terms of exports from developing countries during the period from 1960 to 1975 was in the form of fuels. Furthermore, a large number of developing countries, as a result of their industrialization policies, have begun to export manufactured goods. For example, during the period from 1965 to 1975, exports of manufactured products from these countries increased by 12.3 percent annually, whereas the same exports from developed countries increased by only 8.8 percent annually.

We may conclude from these figures that through the 1980s all the developing countries will be faced with an ever-increasing need for external resources. At the same time, the possibilities of obtaining these resources from their traditional exports will be reduced, and consequently they will have to depend increasingly on income derived from the export of manufactured goods. However, this solution is not without serious limitations due to the protectionist trends that are arising in the industrialized countries.

Mexico views with grave concern this recent resurgence of protectionist policies on the part of the countries that motivate world trade. The World Bank's Report on World Development has noted a marked increase in protectionism among the industrialized countries, and there are strong pressures to adopt further measures. These pressures are partially derived from the continued slow growth of the industrialized nations and the high rates of unemployment that accompany this slow growth.

They are also partially the result of the fact that the developing countries have concentrated their increasing exports in relatively few categories of manufactured products.

Protectionism has led to the application of a wide range of measures: orderly market agreements, import quotas, minimum price levels for imported goods, "voluntary" export restrictions, countervailing duties, administrative obstacles to imports, and subsidies to industries to maintain production levels above and beyond those justified by demand. Petitions have been formulated to control market participation on regional or worldwide bases and to extend protection to include a wider range of products. All these measures adversely affect exports from the developing countries. Quantitative restrictions and market participation agreements directly limit their sales to the industrialized countries, whereas subsidies to weak industries in the industrialized countries limit such sales indirectly.

It is useful to point out that studies made by prestigious research institutions in the United States and Europe and by the World Bank itself bring to light the fact that the manufactured products of the developing countries account for a mere 1.8 percent of the total of manufactured goods consumed by the developed countries. It is obvious, then, that unemployment in these countries cannot be the result of that miniscule 1.8 percent, but rather the result of changes in demand and in the technology of the developed countries. Thus the share of the developing countries in the world trade of manufactured goods provides no justification for the very negative effects that will come about with the application of protectionist measures by the industrialized world.

Mexico's trade with the developed countries was founded and developed on the sale of raw materials, seasonal products (fruits and vegetables), and certain other articles that found a ready market because of their high manual labor content. In exchange, Mexico bought consumer products from the developed countries. However, as Mexico attained greater industrialization, its demand for imports and its exportable supply altered. Mexican imports gradually became concentrated on industrial inputs and machinery, while its exports began to acquire greater added value, thereby strengthening the manufacturing sector.

The origin of Mexico's deficit in its trade relations with the developed countries over the past thirty-five years may be found in its traditionally high growth rates, which have made it necessary to increase its industrial imports. However, in the last fifteen years the trade deficit has become even more acute, owing, among other reasons, to the periodic restrictive measures taken by the developed countries in accordance with the expansion or contraction of their economies. Thus the recent economic recession, which began in 1972 and 1973 and from which the economies of the developed countries have not yet fully recovered, revived their protectionist sentiments and has had negative effects on Mexican exports. I would mention, as an example, that in October 1978 claims were initiated by the United States against Mexican textiles (countervailing duties) and tomatoes (anti-dumping taxes).

In order to achieve efficient trade, it is necessary for the industrialized countries to stop protecting their inefficient industries, particularly when they are incapable of competing with similar enterprises in the developing countries. Their policy of restricting imports of goods that may be detrimental to inefficient industries and may bring about unemployment actually transfers unemployment to the developing countries that are exporting such goods. As a result, the developing countries pay the cost of maintaining employment in their own inefficient industries. For this reason, it is crucial that the governments of the developed countries begin to relocate workers who are in inefficient sectors to sectors in which the developed countries are competitive. This will make it possible for trade to function on the basis of efficiency; it will prevent the trade deficits of the developing countries from becoming still more serious and will obviate the need for these countries to have recourse to foreign debt. Finally, such relocation will make it possible for the cost of allocating resources to be paid by the developed countries and not the developing countries.

Mexico has participated actively in the multilateral trade negotiations taking place in Geneva to formulate a more effective and equitable trade system. Mexico has made concrete suggestions with regard to the content of the various codes that have been proposed, and it has pointed out the pitfalls that should be avoided. Nevertheless, as the date set for concluding these negotiations approached—December 15, 1978—certain questions remained that were of concern to us. One source of anxiety was the proposal that would authorize countries to apply protective measures in a selective manner. Another was the possible application of provisional measures unilaterally, and still another the idea of the developed countries of applying graduated clauses to all the developing countries to deprive them of preferential treatment and increase their obligations. It is unacceptable to include clauses that compel the nonindustrialized nations to ensure access to the supply of goods considered vital by the developed countries. Finally, the draft codes of conduct being negotiated were essentially drawn up by the developed countries and did not adequately grant special and differentiated treatment to the developing countries, nor did they envision the means of ensuring additional benefits for the international trade of these countries, as was stipulated in Tokyo upon the initiation of the negotiations.

Mexico is willing to negotiate any agreement that will equitably regulate world trade for all and thereby ensure the stability required for international transactions to expand at a rapid pace and for the general benefit. However, any such agreement must reflect the principles established in Tokyo.

The enormous needs of the countries of intermediate development, the limited possibilities they have of balancing their trade deficits, and the danger they face of new protectionist policies are all leading them to seek additional sources of financing. At the end of 1976, the public debt of the developing countries that did not produce oil amounted to $140 billion. The medium- and long-term private debt of these countries amounted to an additional $30 billion, and the short-term debt amounted to $50 billion. That is, the overall foreign debt was on the order of $220 billion. In 1977, this debt was estimated at approximately $250 billion. Between 1970 and 1977, the foreign debt of these countries increased by 270 percent.

The World Bank estimates that by 1985 the needs of developing countries for external financing will increase by 338 percent over that of 1975. It is also estimated that more than half of these needs will be required solely for the purpose of financing external debt service. This means that the debt coefficient—that is, the debt service as a percentage of the income obtained from the export of goods and services—will increase from 11.8 percent in 1975 to 21 percent in 1985.

The sources of the external resources obtained by the developing countries in 1975 were as follows: 16 percent was derived from official aid, 19 percent from concessionary credits, and 65 percent from private credits at prevailing market interest rates. However, the sources of such resources for the countries of intermediate development showed a different pattern: 12 percent came from official aid, 14 percent from concessionary credits, and 74 percent from private credits at prevailing market interest rates. By 1985, it is estimated that these countries will obtain 78 percent of their external resources from private banking at market terms and interest rates.

This means that over the next ten years, these countries will have to increase the volume of external resources for their development by 300 percent, and they will have to obtain these resources from private banking under nonconcessionary terms. The result will be such an increase of the debt service burden that the debt service coefficient will rise from its present 12 percent to an estimated 22 percent in 1985. This implies that the debt service coefficient will rise from the present 2.7 percent of the gross domestic product of these countries to 4.8 percent in 1985.

Obviously, the situation I have described will affect the growth rates of the economies of the developing countries. Moreover, it will result in less growth for the developed countries since 25 percent of the exports of the developed countries is destined for the countries of intermediate development. A slower pace of growth in these countries will diminish their purchases from the developed world.

The financial requirements of almost all the countries of intermediate development must increase if they are to alleviate already existing social and economic tensions. To think in terms of using the private banking system as a means of covering these needs is to ignore the obvious insufficiency of long-term financial resources. It would also postpone low-yield projects of a social nature and overlook the great need for capital goods.

Thus the strengthening of international financial institutions and their adaptation to new needs is a vital task. By ensuring that these institutions perform their function of transferring real resources to nonindustrialized and semi-industrialized countries, we can guarantee the replacement and progressive increase of their capital, thereby creating an increasing flow of financing for development. The World Bank, for example, should give priority to the urgent problems of the international economy and grant clear-cut preference to the weakest countries. But at the same time it should evolve and transform itself into the International Development Bank and channel an increasing portion of its resources to all the developing economies.

For Mexico, international financial organizations play a key role in obtaining and supplying financial and technical resources, a task that cannot be performed properly by means of bilateral or private mechanisms. We support measures taken to increase the World Bank's capital that will at the same time maintain an annual growth rate in its loans of between 7 and 9 percent. This may be instrumental in alleviating the problems presented by the reduction in official aid and the stagnation of world trade, which have gradually compelled the developing countries to concentrate their foreign debts in increasingly burdensome credits.

The International Monetary Fund can and must play an important role in solving the problems faced by the developing countries. The Fund must provide for generous allocation of special drawing rights that will ensure the system's liquidity. Furthermore, quotas concerning the growth of trade should be increased; operation of the supplementary facility (the Witteveen Fund) should be initiated for all the developing countries; and the availability of complementary financing should be expanded.

Mexico is aware of the need for an international financing

system that will promote an efficient flow of goods, services, and capital among the countries making up the international community, a system that will contribute to the orderly and accelerated growth of the world economy. We believe, however, that efficiency cannot and should not be measured strictly on the basis of quantitative criteria. There should be a serious attempt to include all the developing countries in the benefits derived from economic growth, and this should be reflected in the agreements and decision-making processes of international organizations, as well as in the daily practices of the developed countries.

The external resources a developing country may obtain through foreign investment are conditioned by two factors: the volume of foreign investment entering the country and the contribution made by foreign investment to the country in net terms. On a worldwide basis, direct foreign investment increased from $158 billion in 1971 to $287 billion in 1976. Approximately 95 percent of direct foreign investment comes from developed countries, and 75 percent of this total is directed toward other developed countries.

In the last ten years there has been a tendency toward reducing foreign investment in the developing countries. This derives from two factors: a concentration of investment in a few sectors and a concentration of investment in certain developing countries. The key element that explains this concentration is income. Generally speaking, this means that the greater the income a developing country has, the larger its market and the greater its attraction for foreign investment. (The exceptions involve access to raw materials and countries that are strategic for certain corporate marketing programs.) Furthermore, the most dynamic sectors in the developing countries are those with the greatest market potential, and consequently these are the most attractive to foreign investment.

Mexico is a country of intermediate development with a relatively high per capita income. It therefore has a very large market that is growing rapidly. Between 1968 and 1978, Mexico received approximately $500 million a year in new direct foreign investment. This investment represents approximately

10 percent of the country's industrial investment, produces 17 percent of its manufactured goods, imports 28 percent of the total of the country's imports, exports 33 percent of the total of manufactured goods, and represents 45 percent of the country's balance of trade deficit.

As a country of intermediate development, Mexico requires external resources, technology, and skilled labor. Nevertheless, it is necessary to establish clearly the role that foreign investment should play in the country's economic, political, and social development—the influence it should or should not have on the kinds of resources the country must import to accelerate and promote its development. It is also necessary to adopt appropriate measures to maintain control over activities that concern development.

The definition of the role that foreign investment should play in a country's development process is essentially a question of general economic policy. However, the experiences of the developing countries, including Mexico, have demonstrated that the presence of transnational corporations has implications of a political, legal, and social nature. For this reason, foreign investment should not be judged solely from the economic standpoint, but also from the standpoint of the overall development strategy of the country in question.

In many cases, foreign investment in Mexico has financed its working capital and the expansion of its productive capacity with internal resources instead of providing financing by means of external resources and/or reinvestment of profits. Moreover, employment opportunities have been limited by the use of capital-intensive technologies that do not recognize the resources of a country with an abundant supply of labor.

These enterprises also have not exported in sufficient quantities, in spite of their available market facilities abroad. Studies show that the proportion of their production set aside for export is similar to that of domestic corporations. Meanwhile, their imports are generally greater than their exports, which naturally influences Mexico's balance of trade and increases our deficit in this area. Finally, it has been observed that remittances abroad by these corporations of interests, royalties, profits, technical assistance payments, and other items surpass their original investments over a period of five or six years, thereby draining a country already lacking in financial resources.

The Law to Promote National Investment and Regulate Foreign Investment, in effect since 1973, stipulates precise standards for the establishment of new foreign investment in Mexico. In the five years that this law has been in force, it has been possible to establish precedents, criteria, and mechanisms to encourage the entry of foreign investment while making sure that it conforms to the needs and interests of the country.

The vision of the world economy during the next ten years that is seen by developing countries is hardly encouraging. For the countries of intermediate development, the picture is even less favorable. We can foresee that protectionist tendencies will be accentuated during the next three or four years, and this in turn will reduce our exports. We can also foresee that in the next decade the countries of intermediate development will need to rely on foreign capital markets to finance their increasing investment requirements. On the one hand, these requirements will increase as a result of the protectionism of the developed countries; on the other, they will be the result of needs inherent in the high investment coefficients that the countries of intermediate development will require to emerge successfully from their transitional stage. It is also forecast that almost 80 percent of these increased financial requirements will have to be satisfied by means of commercial credit obtained from private banking. This means obtaining resources under unfavorable conditions and at high cost, which not only will affect the capacity of these countries to carry out their development programs, but also will be especially detrimental to their social programs. Finally, it may be observed that foreign investment is being increasingly directed toward the developed countries and to the most dynamic sectors of the economies of the countries of intermediate development. This reduces the volume of resources available for the latter.

Should these tendencies continue, they will bring about a situation in which the countries of intermediate development will be incapable of achieving satisfactory rates of growth. This will result not only in the impoverishment and deterioration of the conditions in which approximately one fifth of the world's inhabitants live, but also in repercussions on the growth rate of the developed countries. The overall result will be a low rate of growth for the world as a whole—for the developed countries, the countries of intermediate development, and the developing countries in general.

It is not my intention to present a vision of catastrophe. My point of departure is only a hypothesis used for the purpose of projecting what may happen over the next few years. We still have time to alter the course of events. To do this, we must initiate change by adopting immediate decisions to prevent a serious crisis in the international economic system. Mexico considers it a necessity—not only for itself, but for the world as a whole—to modify the traditional systems of trade, financing, and foreign investment on the international level. We believe that it is imperative to construct a new economic order that will make reallocation of resources possible, not only in a more efficient but also in a more equitable manner. The results of such change can only benefit the entire international community.

Mexico's Relations with the Third World: Experiences and Perspectives

Olga Pellicer de Brody

Before discussing Mexico's relations with the Third World, it is useful to remember that for a long time our foreign policy was restricted mainly to our dialogue with the United States and to the maintenance of our position within the inter-American system, preoccupations that were quite different from those of other nations in Latin America. Indeed, it was not until the early sixties that Mexico assigned any importance to relations with other developing countries.

This reserved attitude can be explained by both internal and external circumstances. For a long time, the U.S. was our most important customer in the international market, and the main or only supplier of capital and technology. At the same time there was a general atmosphere of distrust produced by the Cold War. In addition, Mexico's political leaders were not particularly interested in international issues. For example, President Ruiz Cortines, "a man of his home," never showed any curiosity about what was going on beyond Mexico's borders. Thus, although a brilliant international diplomat, Luis Padilla Nervo, was foreign minister between 1952 and 1958, Mexican participation in international relations remained quite limited. Our activities in the United Nations were moderate, and our foreign relations focused on the United States.

This situation began changing in the early sixties as the deterioration of Mexican-U.S. trade relations forced Mexican leaders to look for a diversification of the country's economic relations. At the same time, events in the international arena encouraged a new orientation of the country's foreign policy. First came the creation of the Latin American Free Trade Association (LAFTA), a development that greatly interested the Mexican government. Second, conditions began to favor the adoption of a more amicable approach to socialist countries, including the People's Republic of China and the U.S.S.R., both of which held exhibits in Mexico City in the early sixties. Third, the nonaligned countries began to mobilize to present their demands in international organizations, providing an essential reference point for all developing countries. And, finally, President López Mateos realized the value of foreign policy as an element of prestige for the Mexican government, giving high priority to foreign relations, trips abroad, and the welcoming of foreign visitors. From a political point of view, López Mateos opened a new era for Mexico's foreign relations.

Unfortunately, the diversification of Mexico's stance toward the international community diminished again with President Díaz Ordaz. From 1964 to 1970, the dominant idea once again was that the concentration of our foreign relations on the United States was a historical inevitability, although not necessarily a negative one. As a consequence, Mexican diplomats discreetly retired from Third World politics, seemingly disinterested in the conflicts of other Latin American countries. This is illustrated by the lack of interest shown by Mexican politicians in the conferences of the "Group of 77" and by Mexico's indifferent attitude toward Peru during its troubles in 1968 with the International Petroleum Company. Seen against this background, President Echeverría's insistence on identifying Mexico with Third World countries, and Mexico's leadership in the establishment of the Charter of Economic Rights and Duties of Nations, can be considered a new stage in Mexican foreign policy.

What caused the adoption of Mexico's Third World policies during the early seventies? There were many reasons, both economic and political, internal and external. The beginning of the decade witnessed a growing trade deficit: large amounts of capital were going abroad as a result of foreign investment activities and heavy payments for the amortization of public external debt. As a result, the balance of payments became one of the severest problems in the Mexican economy. These circumstances, together with the growing protectionism of the United States, impelled Mexico to search for a diversification of the country's external economic relations and for an alliance with other developing countries in order to improve their joint position in trade negotiations with the United States.

But while economic issues were important components of the new policy, they cannot be considered its only cause. International realities also invited a reappraisal of Mexico's stance. Several Latin American countries, traditionally in favor of U.S. interests, began international negotiations that were characterized by an aggressive nationalism. Within this atmosphere, the application of the principle of nonintervention, or the establishment of diplomatic relations with Cuba, was not enough to maintain the international prestige of the Mexican government. To assure this prestige required nothing less than a new offensive in foreign policy. This direction was even more attractive in view of the other goals of the Echeverría administration, such as the renewal of the official ideology, the consolidation of the public image of the President, and the reconciliation of the latter with the various intellectual groups exerting influence during the late sixties. Another factor was the massive student repression of 1968, in response to concerted criticism of the regime by students and intellectuals. Thus economic problems, the international atmosphere, and the nation's politics all blended together to influence the Mexican government's international activity in a course that perfectly matched the style of a President fascinated by the prospect of an international platform.

What were the goals of this new foreign policy? If the success of a foreign policy is to be measured by prestige, or by the degree of mobilization of public opinion around certain topics, there can be no doubt that the new foreign policy accomplished its aims. Mexico's efforts to focus international public opinion on the unjust distribution of benefits through international trade and on the participation of transnational enterprises in the internal life of developing countries, as well as its lobbying for the approval of the Charter of Economic Rights and Duties of Nations, all represented significant achievements, steps toward strengthening the case of less developed countries in international politics.

Nonetheless, the success of a foreign policy cannot be judged solely in terms of prestige. After all, the real justification of Mexico's international activity should be the amelioration of trade deficits, the reduction of the public debt, and the establishment of a more equitable dialogue with the United States. From this perspective, Mexico's foreign policy from 1970 to 1976 had few successes. At the same time, the economic crisis at the end of 1976 and the devaluation of the peso after twenty-two years of stability placed Mexico in a vulnerable position vis-à-vis the United States government and North American economic groups.

These circumstances would seem enough to discredit Third World politics. Nonetheless, before discrediting the Third World as an instrument for improving Mexico's international relations, it is necessary to pose two questions: Are there any particular circumstances in Mexico's international relations that limit the validity of the Third World alliance? And would it be valid to say that, in light of those circumstances, it is better for Mexico to practice a bilateral foreign policy, to concentrate on the United States?

It is well known that since the end of World War II, Mexican foreign trade has been characterized by its concentration on the United States. Even now, after many efforts to diversify that trade, 60 percent of our exports still go to the U.S. For a long time, those exports were composed mainly of agricultural products, raised and processed in Mexico under the influence of Northern American demand and in close coordination with North American entrepreneurs. For example, it is common for Mexican farmers and cattle raisers to plan their activities with North American entrepreneurs who operate in border states. We should not forget that many Mexican products are produced for export to the U.S., and that North Americans help to finance their production and distribution all over the country. Naturally, Mexican producers and exporters engaged in this activity are not enthusiastic about trade policies proposed and backed by Third World organizations. Alliances to raise prices in the world market or groups to lobby for preferential treatment are of no interest to them. Thus if we analyze this situation from different points of view, we must conclude that some Mexican exporters consider themselves as a functioning part of the U.S. economy.

Another issue that must be considered in relation to the Third World alliance and Mexico's foreign trade is the fact that, as a result of geographic closeness, Mexico has become the only foreign supplier to the U.S. of foodstuffs such as tomatoes, strawberries, and melons. It is obvious that in these areas Mexico would not receive any benefits from an alliance of producers, a typical instrument of Third World organization.

I have presented these examples to emphasize the special nature of the relations existing between Mexico and the U.S. Because of the fact that we are neighbors, it is difficult for Mexico to achieve significant progress in its existing trade relations through alliances with other developing countries.

Keeping all this in mind, one must ask whether it is convenient for Mexico to stay within the Third World camp in the international arena. The answer is yes, for several reasons. First, it is important to remember that the atmosphere created by Third World policies and ideals benefits all developing countries. For example, today it is difficult for the U.S. to take measures that openly oppose Mexican exports because such an action would have political consequences, because it would be widely criticized by Third World countries in every international forum.

It is also important to point out that oil represents one of Mexico's main exports, and in oil transactions we are protected by the existence of a Third World organization, OPEC. It is true that the complexity of our trade relations with the United States makes Mexico's participation in OPEC difficult. Nevertheless, thanks to this organization we can set the most convenient prices and we can obtain considerable benefits from our oil. All this helps to assure a respectful attitude toward oil-producing countries. OPEC gives dignity to countries like Mexico that are forced to export their natural resources.

All these factors show that in spite of the apparent failures of Third World policies during the Echeverría administration, and despite the particular links that accentuate our trade dependence on the United States, the Third World alliance, created for the defense of interests vis-à-vis the so-called industrialized world, will continue to be a reference point that Mexico will use to maintain its position in the international arena.

The Structural Context of U.S.-Mexican Relations

Mario Ojeda Gómez

U.S.-Mexican relations have become a fashionable subject of discussion in the United States. The mass media have greatly expanded their coverage of the subject, and each year more and more universities organize seminars dealing either with Mexican affairs or with the relationship between the United States and Mexico. Today it is common to hear average citizens express opinions about what should be done on matters involving the two countries. There is also no doubt that Mexican affairs and U.S.-Mexican relations have advanced greatly within the scale of priorities of the U.S. government and the U.S. Congress. For example, in 1977, a congressional committee organized a special series of hearings on recent developments in Mexico and their implications for the United States.

This sudden interest in U.S.-Mexican relations can be traced to some important developments that affect the formerly peaceful and routine interaction of the two countries. It seems to me that a number of issues are involved, including drugs, undocumented workers, and the stability of the Mexican state. But the one that has awakened the most interest in Mexico within the United States is Mexico's new potential as an oil-producing nation.

The problem of drug traffic has greatly disturbed U.S.-

Mexican relations. According to U.S. Congress figures, Mexico is the United States' main supplier of heroin and marijuana. During the Nixon administration, the U.S. took the view that the Mexican authorities were not acting as a friendly government since they were doing nothing to stop drug production and the export of drugs to the United States. Consequently, in order to force the Mexican government's hand, Washington decided to apply what in the words of President Nixon was a "shock treatment." Operation Intercept, a scrupulous examination by U.S. customs officers of every traveler entering the United States, was the result. Naturally, Operation Intercept greatly discouraged travel by citizens of both countries, and it affected tourism and the economy of the Mexican border cities. But the economy on the U.S. side also suffered, and the affected groups pressured Washington to end the program.

In fact, Operation Intercept was stopped once the Mexican government agreed to take drastic measures to fight drug and marijuana production, as well as smuggling. Thus the shock treatment succeeded, and Operation Intercept was replaced by Operation Cooperation. Subsequently, the Mexican government, with assistance from the U.S. government, launched a huge campaign to destroy the marijuana fields, which became known as Operation Condor. However, despite this joint effort, large amounts of Mexican drugs, as well as drugs from other countries, still enter the United States. Unfortunately, this will continue to be the case as long as there is a demand for them.

I should say, incidentally, that the antidrug campaign has not occurred without cost to Mexico. The U.S. government has granted cooperation mainly in the form of modern equipment, such as helicopters, but the cost of recruiting hundreds of new narcotics agents, as well as the cost of sending Mexican army troops to the mountains, has been financed by the Mexican government. However, it is undoubtedly the political and social costs that have been the most important to Mexico. For example, it is a well-known fact that whenever smugglers know in advance that their chances of passing through the border are low, they dump their merchandise in Mexico, creating a new market by artificial means. So it is, ironically, that the more successful the antismuggling campaign, the more extended the use of drugs becomes in Mexico itself.

Another issue that became a source of concern for the U.S. government and for interest groups in North America was the economic and political crisis that developed in Mexico following the 1976 devaluation of the peso. One reason for this concern was the destabilizing effect that the crisis could have had on the newly elected government of Mexico and on the political system in general. Obviously, for the United States, as for any country in the world, it is very important to have stable and friendly neighbors. In addition, the devaluation of the peso and the recession of the Mexican economy posed a threat to trade, tourism, and migration. For example, there was fear among businessmen on the U.S. side of the border that the devaluation of the peso would greatly reduce tourism from Mexico and exports to Mexico. The problem was considered to be so important that the United States Congress decided to hold a series of special hearings on the subject. These congressional hearings reached a conclusion that we have known in Mexico for a long time: since the United States is the principal trade partner of Mexico, it follows that any reduction in the Mexican capacity to import goods and services will have a negative effect on U.S. exports.

Despite the importance of drug smuggling and the stability of the peso, the two major issues in present-day relations between Mexico and the United States are undocumented Mexican outmigration and the increased Mexican potential in oil and gas. (The latter has attracted more attention and interest in U.S. government circles and among the general public.) Since these two topics will be dealt with in the chapters that follow, I will not comment on them here. I should point out, however, that the four issues I have mentioned are the ones emphasized by North American perceptions of U.S.-Mexican relations. This is not to say that these concerns are not important from a Mexican perspective. It means only that in Mexico we also tend to emphasize other aspects of our relationship, aspects that are less important to a powerful nation.

This brings me to another way of looking at the United

States and Mexico. In dealing with the subject of foreign relations or bilateral relations, we should distinguish between the structure and the process—in other words, between the political framework within which the relationship take place and the issues or problems that arise from that relationship. The structure within which U.S.-Mexican relations take place includes a number of features, which I will attempt to explain in the following sections.

Territorial contiguity. From a geopolitical perspective, it can be said that to be a contiguous neighbor of the most powerful country on earth means to belong to the sphere of influence of that country. Moreover, it means that the neighboring country constitutes a critical part of the major power's first line of national defense. There are many examples in history that demonstrate this assertion.

According to Hanson Baldwin, author of *Strategy for Tomorrow* and a former *New York Times* expert on strategy, the globe can be divided into five regions according to their degree of priority to the national security of the United States: categorically imperative, vital, very important, of interest, and of low importance. Mexico is located within the first priority: categorically imperative. This means that Mexico is not free to enter into alliances with any country in the world. Additionally, it means that the Mexican government has to be on good terms with Washington; otherwise it risks the danger of being subverted or destabilized from the outside. Finally, and more important, it also means that the very type of political system, as well as the basic policies taken by the Mexican government, have to be agreeable to Washington.

Not all of the consequences of territorial contiguity, however, are negative. On the positive side, it means that Mexico traditionally has had one of the lowest per capita military expenditures. Too weak to fight a war with her northern neighbor and much more powerful than her southern neighbors, Mexico has had no need to expand her military forces for external reasons. And since an attack on Mexico from an extracontinental power would certainly trigger the intervention of the United States, it could be said that Mexico has enjoyed a kind of free ride, thanks to U.S. national security interests. Another benefit derived from Mexico's strategic value is that it has in a certain way strengthened the country's bargaining position vis-à-vis the United States. However, on balance these advantages do not compensate for the limitations on full sovereignty that are imposed by Mexico's proximity to a superpower.

Asymmetry of power. The U.S.-Mexican relationship is an asymmetrical one—that is, Mexico is the weaker partner. The United States is a colossus of over 200 million people. In 1972, it had a GNP of well over $100 billion and a per capita income of $5,590. In contrast, Mexico is a medium-sized nation of 70 million people, with a GNP of about $40 billion and a per capita income of $750. The net consequence of being the weaker partner in the relationship has meant that Mexico has had to accept many of the unilateral decisions taken by Washington.

Economic and technological dependence. From a quantitative perspective, foreign trade is not a very important component of Mexico's economy since it represents about 13 percent of the GNP. However, from a qualitative point of view, imports are very important to the Mexican economy. Most of Mexico's imports consist of capital and semiprocessed goods that are vital to the country's industry. Mexico pays for these imports with raw materials and some manufactured goods. Since industry has become the leading sector of the economy, it follows that any limitation on Mexico's capacity to import tends to have a negative impact on the rate of growth of the Mexican economy as a whole.

Nearly 70 percent of Mexico's imports come from the United States, and about the same percentage of our exports go to the United States. Under these circumstances, any protectionist limitations imposed by Washington on Mexican exports tend to have an almost automatic and a very immediate impact on Mexico's general economy. The same situation exists for both tourism and foreign investment.

From a quantitative point of view, foreign investment plays only a minor and complementary role in Mexico, at least in comparison with other countries. The total value of direct foreign investment in Mexico is approximately $3 billion, of which about 80 percent comes from the United States. This foreign investment contribution amounts to approximately 13 percent of Mexico's total economic production, a very low figure indeed. From a qualitative point of view, however, the role played by foreign investment in the Mexican economy is a very important one. Foreign investment has tended to concentrate in manufacturing and tourism, traditionally the two most dynamic sectors of the Mexican economy. It has been calculated that 65 percent of U.S. investment in Mexico operates in manufacturing.

On the other hand, within Mexican industry itself, foreign investment has tended to be concentrated in the most dynamic and strategic branches. According to a recent study, 26 percent (234) of the 900 largest industrial enterprises in Mexico belongs to foreign capital. But among the 100 largest enterprises 47 percent belongs to foreigners. In addition, foreign enterprises tend to be concentrated among those industries that require sophisticated technology. According to the same study, 53 percent of Mexican enterprises engaged in the production of capital goods are owned by foreigners.

To conclude, from the Mexican perspective it is the structure rather than the process that is the principal concern in our relations with the United States. In other words, the structure of the relationship is what prevents us from being able to negotiate on an equal basis with the United States and what makes it difficult for us to refuse unilateral decisions made in Washington.

Facts, Perceptions, and the Issue of Undocumented Immigration

Jorge Bustamante

The phenomenon of Mexican migration to the United States is the result of a set of interacting factors on both sides of the border. On the Mexican side, we can summarize these factors in the single word "underdevelopment." This term includes unemployment, poverty, patterns of population growth, and a complex domestic situation that is related not only to indigenous developments, but also to Mexico's proximity to the United States. On the United States side, the chief factor is the demand for cheap labor.

The interaction of these forces creates the factual reality of undocumented immigration of Mexican workers to the United States. I use the word "factual" because I think it is important to distinguish between the factual dimension of undocumented immigration, which is the result of what we have been able to learn in our studies and research, and what I call the perceptual dimension, which is the way people have defined the phenomenon. There is an important and serious difference between the two. In the empirical dimension, we should begin with a humble recognition of ignorance. When it comes to this phenomenon, what we don't know is more significant than what we know. Nevertheless, the studies that have been conducted in the last decade have at least given us a clearer picture of the undocumented immigrant: his basic characteristics, his age, his level of education, and the parts of Mexico from which he comes.

Mexican undocumented immigrants go to the United States to work in jobs that pay very low wages and require low skills. They go to the United States and pay taxes and social security. They go to the United States and generally do not use the public services. They go to the United States on a temporary basis. All these facts have been learned by researchers in both the United States and Mexico. However, these findings have not received enough attention to counter the overwhelming North American perception of Mexican undocumented immigrants as a threat, as a silent invasion. This is one of the most serious problems we face in dealing with the issue of undocumented immigration, a problem that we do not seem to be solving with research activities or with the rich data we have accumulated on the history of this phenomenon.

Undocumented immigration is not a recent development, and negative reaction to the presence of undocumented Mexican immigrants in the United States is not new either. In fact, one can find certain recurring patterns in its history. Ever since the end of the First World War, we find that in periods of high unemployment in the United States the issue of Mexican immigration comes to public attention. First there is a situation of unemployment, then Mexican immigration receives more attention from the mass media, and finally the Mexican immigrant is used as a scapegoat for the unemployment that exists in certain regions of the United States, if not throughout the entire country. We find evidence of this particular pattern after the Great Depression. In those years the economic crisis in certain areas was blamed on the Mexican immigrant, resulting in repression, restrictive immigration policies, and eventually in mass deportation. It is important to point out that this pattern ends when the U.S. economy recovers. Then the Mexican immigration issue fades away, along with other concomitant issues, particularly unemployment.

A situation similar to that which I have just described took place after the Second World War, and an even clearer recurrence appeared after the Korean War. It is amazing to see the similarity of reactions during these periods. Today we hear such terms as the "silent invasion," while in previous decades it was the "wetback invasion." Documentaries on the major networks used this theme in a recurring pattern, beginning in early 1954. During the same period, *The New York Times* gave record coverage to Mexican immigration—in six months there were more articles than had appeared in the previous twenty years. Following this media exposure, there was an outcry on the part of the U.S. public against the presence of the Mexican immigrants; there was pressure on policymakers in favor of restrictive measures; and finally there was the infamous "Operation Wetback" in 1954, in which more than a million people were apprehended.

We do not seem to have learned from this history. Indeed, in the late 1970s the pattern appeared again. Naturally, it is frustrating not to be able to break this cycle, to continue to produce conditions that prevent reasonable dialogue and reasonable negotiations to find a solution to this common problem. The interaction of economic, social, cultural, and labor realities does not start or finish at the border; it permeates both our countries.

The result is a situation in which the phenomenon of undocumented immigration seems drastically different when viewed, on the one hand, from the perspective produced by our research and, on the other, from the perspective of the U.S. public as it is shaped by newspapers and television. What happens is that North American perceptions call for definitions that become not factual but political. This is what is happening to Mexican immigrants in the United States. They have been defined as a threat, and so they are treated as a threat.

Thus the role that the Mexican undocumented immigrant plays in the U.S. economy is totally unrecognized by the U.S. public. The extent to which the presence of these immigrants affects prices, in fact helps to maintain lower prices, is unrecognized. The fact that these immigrants are paying taxes and social security and are not receiving benefits from these payments is also unrecognized. As a result, a perception of the situation that is not based on facts prevails, and is reflected in the measures and policies designed in the United States to deal with Mexican immigration.

One could say, of course, that these policies are not designed specifically to counter the Mexican immigration phenomenon, but rather to deal with undocumented immigration from any country. This is a very fine distinction—when we speak of un-documented immigration policies, in reality we are speaking of policies that will mainly affect Mexican immigration. This is not to say that undocumented immigration from other countries is stable. In fact, recent data have shown that it is increasing, par-ticularly on the East Coast of the United States. However, the important point to be made here is that in this situation a large phenomenon has been defined in political rather than empirical terms.

In this regard I should say that Mexico is also at fault be-cause we have not come up with better data. In Mexico there is also a political definition of the phenomenon, one that sees un-documented immigration as an escape valve, which is as falla-cious as defining Mexican immigration as a threat. Thus what we have now are two government policies based on political rather than factual definitions. It is, therefore, necessary to find a rea-sonable basis on which we can discuss the facts of this phenome-non on its own terms.

It is not by chance that we see Mexican immigrants coming through many holes, in spite of new fences along the U.S./Mexi-can border. Interestingly enough, we Mexicans do not have the same reaction when we see our capital going through similar holes. We have certain ideas about undocumented immigration, but we do not have the same ones about the undocumented capital that is leaving the country in violation of our domestic laws. We do not seem to find these situations comparable.

Perhaps this is true because we lack an understanding of the impact that the Mexican immigrant is having and will continue to have on the U.S. economy. For example, some economists have suggested that perhaps the only way the retirement system in the United States will be financed is through Mexican immigrants who are paying their social security dues and their taxes.

To conclude, then, the main point I wish to make is that one obligation shared by the United States and Mexico is the need to begin a reasonable dialogue in order to find solutions to our common problems.

A Mexican-U.S. Energy Market: The Conflict of Interests

Samuel I. del Villar

Along with the U.S. demand for Mexican labor and Mexico's overall structural trade deficit with the United States, the emergence of a Mexican-U.S. energy market has become a key issue in the relationship between the two countries. We can speak of a Mexican-U.S. energy market not only because Mexico has an oil surplus and is willing to sell, but also because the United States has an oil shortage and must therefore buy abroad. There are also economic and political factors that tend to solidify this market still further. Mexican crude oil is of high quality. In addition, due to its proximity, Mexico has a competitive advantage in supplying hydrocarbons (particularly natural gas) to the United States. This situation has been greatly influenced by the decline of other producers in the Western Hemisphere, namely Venezuela and Canada.

In the United States, conservation programs have proven to be quite ineffective in reducing the rate of growth in the demand for energy, and North American consumers seem to be highly reluctant to endure burdens imposed by Congress. The result is an ever-increasing reliance on foreign energy sources, a reliance that in the long run might prove to be dangerous and destablizing.

According to U.S. national security definitions, Mexico

121

should be the most reliable foreign source of energy. After all, no other foreign supplier—current or potential—is nearer to the United States than Mexico, and there is no foreseeable risk that other foreign powers might build up vested interests that could threaten Mexico's ability to control its energy reserves. In addition, Mexico enjoys a constitutional system whose stability and endurance compare favorably not only with Third World and Latin American countries, but even with leading industrial nations such as Germany, France, Spain, and Italy. Stable constitutional processes have characterized Mexican polity for more than fifty years. Even now, despite the most severe economic crisis in the last thirty-five years (and amid the superficial rhetoric about political violence that it awakened in 1976, especially in the U.S. press), there are no indications that orderly political processes could be threatened in the foreseeable future. The electoral reform enacted in 1978, which grants greater political participation to opposition parties on the left and right, has only increased the political representation of the system, thereby enlarging its democratic support. It would appear, then, that under these circumstances, the stage would be set for Adam Smith's "invisible hand," organizing a significant Mexican-U.S. energy market. But this has not been the case. Instead, there seems to be a basic conflict of national interests that stands in the way.

The world energy market has become highly regulated. Oligopolistic pricing by private cartels has been replaced by a complex scheme that includes a combination of the governments of oil-exporting countries, the oil companies, and the governments of the industrial oil-importing nations. The U.S. domestic market is itself a highly regulated one. Prices are ultimately fixed by the political process, which is primarily concerned with subsidizing consumption, despite the administration's efforts to ration the use of energy through the tax system. This regulatory scheme, and the alleged North American national interest that it seeks to satisfy, is an important barrier to integrating the Mexican-U.S. energy market.

The United States has sought to ensure a very cheap source of supply at the expense of Mexican hydrocarbon reserves. This attitude is, of course, economically rational to the extent that it embodies a national effort to increase domestic welfare, even if it comes at the expense of the welfare of an important trade partner. And there are reasons to believe that the U.S. government could coerce Mexico into entering arrangements of this sort. In 1978, Mexico emerged from a severe economic crisis in which a very substantial trade deficit drained the country's reserves and its possibilities of real per capita economic growth. It should be pointed out that the United States benefited enormously from this deficit. Between 1970 and 1977, the Mexican economy lost about $10 billion to the U.S., even considering the remittances of Mexican workers in the U.S. The North American energy policy has sought to take advantage of these circumstances by attempting to impose conditions on the financial support Mexico needs both to deal with the short-run crisis and to exploit the country's hydrocarbon reserves. The United States would, above all, like to see long-term agreements, which tend to freeze prices.

Mexican national interest runs exactly in the opposite direction. While Mexico has appeared to be quite cooperative (for example, it has openly stated its refusal to participate in OPEC or to abide by its quotas), this does not mean that an accelerated exploitation of reserves at a low price is in accordance with Mexican national interest or that the Mexican government is prepared to entertain this kind of arrangement.

Mexico's international energy policy is guided by three basic concerns. First, hydrocarbon exports should not subsidize the deficit on the current account of the balance of payments. Second, hydrocarbon reserves should not be rapidly depleted since this would pose a very serious threat to Mexico's development (the country is not prepared to shift toward alternative sources of energy). Third, hydrocarbon reserves are to be considered a national patrimony that should ensure the long-term welfare of the Mexican people. Thus these basic concerns run contrary to U.S. policy. Clearly, Mexico is not prepared to use its oil reserves to subsidize U.S. consumption at the expense of Mexicans—who are, after all, much worse off than North Americans.

It is true that the Mexican bargaining position was severely weakened by the crisis from 1976 to 1977 and that an accelerated exploitation and exportation program was in fact put into effect. However, this program was not intended to satisfy the U.S., but rather to meet domestic energy demand and obtain sufficient international liquidity to finance a reasonable economic growth rate. Petróleos Mexicanos (PEMEX), the state-owned oil company, embarked on an investment program designed to enable the nation to reach a production platform of 2.25 million barrels a day by 1980. At that point, the government will determine future levels of production and exportation.

The conflict between Mexican and U.S. energy policies has already become apparent in the case of the sale of natural gas. On the basis of an agreement with six North American companies to pay $2.65 per thousand cubic feet, PEMEX committed itself to undertake the monumental construction of a pipeline to carry 2 billion cubic feet of natural gas per day to the U.S. from Mexico's southeastern oil fields. However, an administrative order, called for by Senator Adlai Stevenson and backed by then Secretary of Energy James Schlesinger, blocked the agreement. They obviously assumed that Mexico's financial troubles, together with its irreversible commitment to build the pipeline, would ultimately force prices even lower, creating a Mexican-U.S. energy market more suitable to U.S. national interests.

But the assumption proved to be wrong. The attempted coercion of the Mexican government ended the negotiations to develop a Mexican-U.S. natural gas market. Instead of giving in on the price, the Mexican government decided not to sell gas to the U.S., but rather to consume the gas domestically and to export fuel oil. At the same time, PEMEX undertook a strenuous effort to diversify its international sales in order gradually to reduce its dependence on the U.S. market for crude oil.

The political consequences in Mexico of the U.S. attitude have damaged the atmosphere needed to integrate the binational energy market. Mexico's decision to export substantial quantities of oil was itself politically very difficult. After all, the basic rationale that had dominated the oil industry since its nationalization in 1938 was to ensure that there would always be enough oil to meet the demands of an industrializing domestic economy to prevent international exploitation of reserves. There was considerable controversy over the PEMEX export program and over the planned construction of the pipeline. The unilateral cancellation of the gas agreement increased Mexico's political antagonism toward accommodating the U.S. market—and, unless the U.S. government is prepared to change its attitude substantially, it will certainly make building future agreements much more difficult.

There are other circumstances that make it very hard to envision further development of the Mexican-U.S. energy market. After all, the exportation of Mexican oil reserves to the United States cannot be viewed as a phenomenon isolated from the general flow of capital, labor, goods, and services between the two countries—and the policies dominating this general flow are highly protective. In Mexico, industrial protectionism has resulted in a manufacturing industry that is not competitive on the international scene. This poses enormous obstacles to the integration of Mexican-U.S. markets of final and some intermediate manufactured products. The U.S. has readily accepted this situation for a number of reasons: the dependence of the Mexican manufacturing plant on the importation of North American technology and goods; the contraband of North American manufacturers; the remittances by U.S. multinational corporations of profits obtained in the protected Mexican market; and the net gain in the balance of trade and services that the United States obtains from Mexican protectionism. On the other hand, in the United States, protectionism has taken the form of an attempt to defend North American unskilled labor against the immigration of unemployed or underemployed Mexicans. Mexico has tolerated this policy, however reluctantly, because of its very limited leverage in the North American political process, and because the undocumented immigration of Mexican labor to the U.S. is fostered by such a policy.

These protectionist measures have become something of a vicious circle. It is impossible for Mexico to liberalize its trade policies if, at the same time, the U.S. does not liberalize its labor policies. The problem is that North American labor policies tend toward an extreme protectionism that disregards even basic human rights. Thus the ultimate goal of such measures would seem to be to build a kind of Berlin wall between Mexico and the United States.

However, it should be evident that this protectionism cannot be the basis for a stable and constructive economic relationship between the United States and Mexico. If the United States—through its labor, financial, and trade policies—continues applying pressure to obtain Mexican oil reserves at the expense of the well-being of Mexicans, the inevitable result will be a growing antagonism between the two societies.

Special Problems and a Not-So-Special Relationship: Mexican Foreign Policy and the United States

Jorge Castañeda

In Mexico, we are told—we tell ourselves—that in order to overcome underdevelopment we must be better prepared, better equipped, better organized, better administered, and better educated so that we can deal effectively with our internal problems, with the United States, and with the world. But our lack of education, our lack of preparedness and organization, is precisely what constitutes underdevelopment. It is a vicious circle with no escape, or at least one from which very few, if any, developing countries have yet escaped. Indeed, authorities such as Gunner Myrdal tell us that we should not try to follow the path that present-day developed countries followed in the nineteenth century to overcome their backwardness because conditions are not the same. We would not succeed in creating a truly modern economy, and in the process we might well destroy our social fabric. Quite frankly, we in Mexico would not like to end up with your North American social fabric as a result of achieving a modern economy.

Each country must find its own path. It is true that we are a bit special; we have petroleum, which will mean money one day. As the saying goes, money does not bring happiness—but it can

127

help. Yet when we look for an example of a backward country, with plenty of oil and money, that has tried to move quickly into the modern developed world, we stumble upon Iran. And Iran is far from an ideal model. Clearly, it is not easy to be a developing country in the second half of the twentieth century.

But then Mexico is not an ordinary developing country: we are the neighbor of the United States. Díaz, who knew about these things, lamented that Mexico was so near to the U.S. and so far from God. I think that our proximity to the United States was our main predicament in the last century, while our underdevelopment better reflects our difficulties in coping with, or even grasping, the complexities and problems as well as the opportunities of the twentieth century.

The purpose of our foreign policy in the earliest days of our independence was merely to help our country survive; later it was necessary to maintain our territorial integrity. At the turn of the century, our goal was to modernize through foreign investment, but without becoming a foreign colony. During the Revolution and after, as we tried to recover our natural resources, our aim was to defend our land reform program and the other essential and deeply felt economic and social changes that had taken place. After the Second World War, in spite of the narrow limits imposed by the Cold War, Mexico tried to maintain a minimum of political independence and to foster externally the accelerated economic growth that took place during the fifties and sixties.

During Echeverría's administration, Mexico followed a more dynamic foreign policy. We looked for new trading partners; tried to diversify our financial and economic relationships; and attempted to establish, solidify, and even institutionalize our links with other developing countries in order to strengthen the concerted action of the Third World. This policy also was meant to provide us with stronger negotiating positions vis-à-vis the United States. In this we failed, simply because of the international reality of the modern world—or, if you wish, because of the power relationships that define it. A good and just cause is often not sufficient to change a status quo that favors the powerful, at least in a brief period. It is true that Echeverría's militant stance, coupled with some errors of judgment, might even have proved counterproductive, alienating friends and potential allies in both the United States and the Third World. Still, this factor must not be exaggerated; the true reasons for Mexico's foreign policy failure are deeper.

What lesson can be drawn from our historical experience? What international objectives should Mexico pursue, and what should be the cornerstone of its present foreign policy? Obviously, for a country like Mexico foreign policy is a function of its internal aims. It would appear inevitable that Mexico will have to depart somewhat from the development model of the fifties and sixties. Mexico will have to place greater emphasis on a fuller mobilization of its work force and a better use of its natural resources by creating labor-intensive activities for the production of goods that are socially and nationally useful. This must be coupled with a serious effort to bring about a better distribution of income, through labor policies and through fiscal measures. Assuming that this objective is realized, and even if it is achieved to a large extent through the resources generated by the sale of oil and gas, the need to import technology and capital goods and to obtain loans will not appreciably diminish for some time. Neither will the need to increase our exports. Thus, for the foreseeable future, the United States will remain our basic source of goods, capital, and technology, as well as our natural market. Likewise, the United States will continue to serve as the safety valve for our surplus labor force.

All these factors—which, taken together, suggest a strong interdependence—lead to the inevitable conclusion that Mexico's relations with the United States are at present the cornerstone of its foreign policy. This is not a matter of preference, desirability, political choice, or long-range inevitability. It is simply a stark reality in the world as it is today. However, the fact that relations with the United States are inevitably the cornerstone of Mexico's foreign policy does not necessarily dictate an excessive and unbearable political, economic, and cultural dependence. I sincerely think that there is room for genuine interdependence in spite of the asymmetry of power. But it depends mainly on Mexico.

In saying this, I discount the possibility of any sudden, newly discovered or rediscovered good will, sympathy, or moral consideration on the part of the United States that could change its basic attitude toward Mexico. The past history of U.S. policy, its present-day prepotency, its selfishness and conservative mood, will not allow for such a change. Great powers will act as great powers. Thus the nature of our mutual relationship depends essentially on Mexico's attitude and conduct. It will hinge on how Mexico manages its assets. And Mexico does have strong political, economic, and material assets that could assure a genuinely interdependent, healthy, and mutually advantageous relationship.

There are a number of ways in which Mexico could enhance its relationship with the United States. The first that logically should be considered is the realization by Mexico that although the United States is a key element in its external relations, it is not the only element. This should seem obvious, but to the rightist groups that reacted adversely to Echeverría's overtures to the Third World, it is not. There is a confusion here between substance and form.

As I suggested earlier, the goal of closing ranks with the Third World is a valid one, and we should continue our efforts to establish and consolidate a new international economic order. If possible, Mexico should be at the forefront of this movement. We know it will be a long and difficult struggle, but it is a just cause. Weak countries have no other choice but to have faith in the value of ideas, and some day these ideas will bear fruit. The Charter of Economic Rights and Duties, proposed by Mexico, was a well-conceived and partially successful first step in that direction. It should be clear, though, that the new economic order is a long-range objective; it cannot replace the daily hard bargaining that takes place with the United States on commercial matters. Nevertheless, this economic objective should be an important element in our foreign policy. Aside from its inherent value, it is a symbol of Mexico's role in the world, a sign of its political independence, and an affirmation of its international personality. These are essential ingredients in the external policy of a country like Mexico. And our economic pursuits can be carried out without seriously affecting our relations with the United States. After all, Mexico has sufficient maturity and international stature not to indulge in the use of unnecessary provocations and irritants.

A more immediate, concrete, and promising means of diminishing our excessive commercial and financial dependence on the United States is to diversify our trading partners, especially in Western Europe, Japan, the socialist countries, and Latin America. The Mexican government is acutely conscious of this goal, as witnessed by President José López Portillo's visits to China, Japan, and the U.S.S.R. in 1978, and to Western Europe and several nations in the Caribbean basin, including Cuba, in 1980. But this is a long-range project, and so far it has only been partially successful. In the case of other developing countries, particularly in Latin America, the possibilities of industrial or commercial joint ventures should be explored further. In general, we should pursue the concept of collective self-reliance in our relations with other developing countries.

In the political field, there are two cases in which closer association with other countries would be worthwhile. In other publications, I have made the point that the inter-American system is neither the natural nor the appropriate legal and political framework for furthering the regional needs of Latin American countries, for the simple reason that it encompasses two parts of the continent whose interests, problems, and regional needs do not often coincide. The Latin American Economic System (SELA) is the first attempt to establish a mechanism for promoting purely Latin American regional interests in the commercial and economic fields. Perhaps we are not ready for a similar trial in the political sphere but at least we should have frequent political consultations in order to reach common positions on political problems whenever possible.

The so-called Tlatelolco Dialogue of 1975 between the United States and the whole of Latin America is an example of the possibilities inherent in closer political cooperation among Latin American nations. In spite of the present political diversity of Latin America, further attempts should be made to formalize these periodic consultations. The round of summit meetings held in 1978 by Latin American heads of state, including President López Portillo, is a good example of this.

Aside from the Latin American community, there is a kind of natural relationship among a number of countries that can be loosely described as medium powers, following to a greater or lesser extent an independent policy on multilateral questions and thus exerting a certain influence in the international arena. Among these countries are Sweden, Canada, Algeria, India, Yugoslavia, Romania, Venezuela, Brazil, and Mexico. The unifying factor here is not nonalignment, although it is a fact that some of these countries often take the same or similar positions on major political problems and on multilateral economic matters. Since each country belongs to other geographical or political groups, no one considers the possibility of a bloc of relatively independent, like-minded intermediate powers. But if they were a bit more conscious of their like-mindedness and became accustomed to consulting among themselves and acting together on an ad hoc basis—as, for instance, Mexico, Sweden, and Yugoslavia often do on disarmament matters—they could, together, carry a certain weight in the resolution of important international problems. I believe that Mexico should try to encourage and organize this type of political cooperation.

Last, but not least, Mexico should cultivate its relations with the socialist countries, not as a simplistic and mechanical counterweight to the influence of the United States, but as a genuine, indispensable part of its foreign policy.

I have mentioned several elements of Mexico's external policy: improved cooperation in the Third World, the search for new trading partners, closer association with other countries in Latin America, common policy with other like-minded nations, and better relations with the socialist states. However, though they are important, they are no substitute for the main concern of Mexico's foreign policy: our relations with the United States.

For the reasons that were stated earlier, our rapport with the United States ranks first in our international relations. Our relationship with the U.S. can and must be based on mutual respect, and it should be as close and cordial as possible. But the friendly and cordial character of these relations must not be seen as an end in itself. Unfortunately, this has not always been the view of some of our statesmen. Our means of action, our attitudes, and even our forms of communication with the United States must not be subordinated to the supreme aim of maintaining friendly relations. Rather, they should be dictated by the imperative of achieving our own objectives.

I hope that no one in Mexico seriously believes anymore in the existence of a "special relationship" between the United States and Mexico. Though this term is undefined, it presumably means a relationship that is not common to other countries, and implies that this relationship is more favorable to Mexico than to other countries. In Mexico, at one time or another, much emphasis was placed on the specially warm and close personal contacts between the high officials of the two countries. It was thought that easy access and a friendly attitude could be decisive factors in obtaining a special or more favorable reaction to a Mexican request. In short, there was assumed to be a relationship similar (though at a proportionately lower level of importance) to that which existed during World War II between the United States and Great Britain, and which, as Great Britain learned to its dismay, ceased to exist when the dust settled. During the 1960s, this "special relationship" between the U.S. and Mexico proved to be a delusion every time it was put to the test: in the cotton dumping, in Operation Intercept, and in the restrictions on the export of meat and tomatoes, to name just a few examples.

More recently, two cases are particularly illustrative of the lack of any special U.S. consideration for Mexico. The first is the reduction in the late 1970s of the immigration quota for Mexicans to the United States. If there is a case where special consideration is warranted, it is this: after all, Mexico is a neighboring country, with a long tradition of substantial emigration to the United States. In addition, the U.S. was aware that the reduction of the quota would have a negative impact on Mexico. Nevertheless, when the United States saw the need for a new general immigration policy (a need that no one disputes), even though its review allowed for an ad hoc examination of each region or country, Mexico not only failed to receive more favorable consideration than others, but actually got comparatively less favorable consideration. Thus our quota was reduced by half, from 40,000 to 20,000 persons annually.

The second case that illustrates the lack of special consideration for Mexico involves trade. In spite of Mexico's preference, and need, to rely on bilateral trade agreements with the United States that might include some trade concessions, the U.S. government has taken the position that trade relations with Mexico should function within a multilateral framework, in spite of the fact that the State Department has on occasion supported Mexico's position. The difference became so great that the United States-Mexico Trade Commission, created in 1965, was practically defunct by 1973 precisely because of the unwillingness of the United States to deal with Mexico on a bilateral or "special" basis.

This reaction was not totally unexpected. If one considers the present North American political reality, the global interests of the United States, and its network of multilateral economic links, it would be unrealistic to assume that the United States would grant Mexico exceptional treatment in the solution of serious problems. The U.S. conception of our bilateral issues is the first obstacle to any such special relationship. The problems of which we talk constantly—illegal migrants, drugs, trade, the sale of oil and gas, and so forth—are not seen as problems for Mexico, but rather as problems for the United States that are caused by Mexico. Even the potential political and economic instability that could occur in Mexico is seen mainly as a problem for the United States.

But what about our problems? Take the case of drugs. I do not read much in the North American press, nor do I hear much on North American radio and television, about the problems caused in Mexico by drug smugglers, pushers, and gangsters (many of them North American) who finance the crops. And this is just part of Mexico's larger problem: having as a neighbor the principal world buyer for drugs, a country that is therefore the chief reason for their production and for the social evils they cause in Mexico.

North Americans call issues like this the "Mexican problem." And until they conceive of them as problems *for* Mexico, not just problems caused by Mexico for the United States, the proper mental and moral framework for a special relationship cannot be established. Our dealings with the United States should not be based on misconceptions.

So much for the special relationship. Every issue will have to be negotiated and, if need be, fought over, without any favors or special consideration granted or expected. Our success in obtaining fair treatment will depend on the merits of our position and on Mexico's ability to use its assets, to play its cards well.

At the moment, this situation is not particularly favorable. Mexico's huge foreign debt, the worldwide inflation, the sluggish recovery of the world economy, the protective and even defensive attitude of many countries on trade and immigration matters, and the conservative mood of the U.S. Congress will all no doubt hinder Mexico's present negotiating position. But some of these factors are of a transitory and circumstantial nature. Our relationship with the United States is permanent. And Mexico does have some permanent negotiating assets.

I would assign the highest importance to one factor: with the passage of time, especially since the oil expropriation in 1938, Mexico has acquired a certain confidence in her capacity to act internationally. The consistent and relatively independent nature of her foreign policy since then is, in itself, a powerful force that will have its bearing in future relations with the United States. The Mexican public has become accustomed to a healthy political nationalism and to seeing Mexico take positions that reveal a certain measure of independence vis-à-vis the United States, at least to a degree that can be favorably compared with most Latin American countries. Thus the effect of an earlier stand has become the basis for the future foreign policy of the country. Mexican public opinion could hardly accept a radical change in this attitude.

A second major asset for present-day Mexico is its proximity to the United States. Proximity means, first and foremost, that Mexico is one of the very few countries in the world that can afford the luxury of not being burdened by the cost of armaments and a large military establishment. As the neighbor of the most powerful military power in the world, it would be senseless for Mexico to acquire arms other than those needed for internal security. To appreciate the enormous savings this represents, one could compare our situation with that of middle-sized or even small countries that live next to a rival of the same size, so that the symmetry in power forces them to outbid each other in armaments: for example, Brazil and Argentina, Argentina and Chile, Chile and Peru. Each of these countries spends as much as three to five times more than Mexico per capita on armaments.

Proximity to the United States also involves a clear economic advantage. After all, being near to the largest and richest market in the world should give us a natural competitive edge in exports. This is certainly true for Mexican oil and gas. Finally, whether you like it or not (and you do not like it), and whether we like it or not (and we do not like it either, though for different reasons), proximity allows us to solve, at least partially, the problem of unemployment in Mexico. To appreciate the importance of this in economic terms, we both should bear in mind that in the last few years about 800,000 Mexicans have managed to cross the border every year and stay in the United States, at least for a temporary job. This figure is about equivalent to the yearly increase of the Mexican labor force. No matter what restrictive measures the United States may adopt, it will continue for some time to come to absorb part of Mexico's excess population.

There are limits to the restrictive policies the U.S. can adopt. We are both conscious that massive deportation could have grave results in Mexico. This is a case where special attention—if not special consideration—will be given in the United States to the risks inherent in the troubled social situation of its neighbor. Here again, proximity may defend rather than threaten us.

On the other hand, some hold the opposite view. They believe that if a situation were to arise in Mexico that could seriously threaten U.S. interests, the very nearness of Mexico would be an inducement for strong intervention. There may be some truth in this, but on the whole I feel that Mexico would be no more or less exposed than any other country within the North

American political orbit. Nearness is not the decisive factor. The people of Vietnam know very well that remoteness is no defense against armed intervention from North America. Allende's Chile was not protected by distance from political intervention. Conversely, Cuba proves that in spite of the importance of U.S. interests mere proximity—the famous ninety miles—did not necessarily lead to an invasion or even to the overthrow of the regime. Clearly, there are limits to the use of power. We would be no better off, and no worse off, than other comparable countries, near or far.

Apart from the two assets I have mentioned—a robust nationalism and proximity to the United States—Mexico also has important material resources, notably oil and gas. In spite of efforts at conservation, the United States' consumption of oil and gas will continue to increase substantially. To meet this demand, Mexico has plentiful proven and probable reserves, a slight edge in transportation costs, and a safe source of supply. We have what you need and, perhaps for a long time, it will be a seller's market.

In a few years, Mexico can follow one of several courses. We can adopt a conservationist approach, as have Canada and Iraq, or we can open and close the valves on the basis of other equally legitimate interests—for instance, the solution of other foreign problems. All these can be powerful negotiating tools.

In view of the weakness of our position on the other two main bilateral issues, migration and trade, the obvious policy would be to link the three issues. If we proceed with imagination and skill, the objective basis of our position could be sufficiently solid to obtain better treatment in trade and migratory matters. However, package deals—that is, linkage of international issues—can be a potent, though risky medicine. To administer it properly will require a clear and cautious vision of Mexico's objectives so as not to overplay our hand. It will also necessitate a good knowledge of the North American political scene, negotiating skill, and, above all, coordinated policy and unified direction of negotiations.

This last requisite is not easy to fulfill. Mexico's tradition and practice in diplomatic negotiation with the United States has not been to deal with several issues in an integrated manner, but rather to approach matters on an ad hoc basis. Furthermore, the Mexican preference seems to be for each issue to be negotiated by a different agency—aside, of course, from the general coordination and direction that comes from the president. A similar practice apparently exists in the United States, at least as far as negotiations with Mexico are concerned. Thus if Mexico wants to improve its negotiating position, it will have to adopt tactics and methods congruent with the nature of the problems.

Notes on Contributors

Ignacio Bernal, an archaeologist, was one of the founders of the National Museum of Anthropology in Mexico City and was also its first director.

Jorge Bustamante is Professor of Sociology at El Colegio de México.

Jorge Castañeda, formerly Professor of International Law at El Colegio de México, is currently Mexico's foreign minister.

Samuel I. del Villar is a professor in the Center of International Studies at El Colegio de México.

Joseph John Jova, President of Meridian House International in Washington, D.C., served as U.S. Ambassador to Mexico from 1974 to 1977.

Porfirio Muñoz Ledo, a former Minister of Education and special advisor to the President of Mexico, is currently Mexico's Ambassador to the United Nations' Security Council.

Mario Ojeda Gómez, a political scientist, is the General Academic Coordinator of El Colegio de México.

Olga Pellicer de Brody, Professor of International Relations at El Colegio de México, is a specialist in Mexican-U.S. relations.

Fernando Pérez Correa is the General Secretary of the National Autonomous University of Mexico.

Rafael Segovia is a political scientist on the faculty of El Colegio de México.

Bernardo Sepúlveda Amor is Director of International Economic Affairs in the Mexican Ministry of Finance.

Rodolfo Stavenhagen is Professor of Sociology at El Colegio de México.

Luis Unikel is Professor of Sociology at El Colegio de México.

Victor L. Urquidi is Director General of El Colegio de México.

Josefina Vásquez, a historian, is Director of the Department of Historical Studies at El Colegio de México.

Other Public Affairs Publications
Sponsored by the
Center for Inter-American Relations/New York

Authoritarianism in Mexico
INTER-AMERICAN POLITICS SERIES, VOLUME 2
José Luis Reyna and Richard S. Weinert, editors
Philadelphia: Institute for the Study of Human Issues

The Americas in a Changing World: Including the Report
of the Commission on United States–Latin American Relations
With a Preface by Sol M. Linowitz
New York: Quadrangle/The New York Times Book Company

Latin America: The Search for a New International Role
SERIES IN LATIN AMERICAN INTERNATIONAL AFFAIRS, VOLUME 1
Ronald G. Hellman and H. Jon Rosenbaum, editors
New York: John Wiley and Sons

International Economic Relations of Latin America
SERIES IN LATIN AMERICAN INTERNATIONAL AFFAIRS, VOLUME 2
Joseph Grunwald, editor
Beverly Hills, Cal.: Sage Publications

The Peruvian Experiment: Continuity and Change Under Military Rule
Abraham F. Lowenthal, editor
Princeton, N.J.: Princeton University Press

Politics of Compromise: Coalition Government in Colombia
R. Albert Berry, Ronald G. Hellman, and Mauricio Solaun, editors
New York: Cyrco Press

Terms of Conflict: Ideology in Latin American Politics
INTER-AMERICAN POLITICS SERIES, VOLUME 1
Morris Blachman and Ronald G. Hellman, editors
Philadelphia: Institute for the Study of Human Issues

Brazil and Mexico: Patterns in Late Development
INTER-AMERICAN POLITICS SERIES, VOLUME 3
Sylvia A. Hewlett and Richard Weinert, editors
Philadelphia: Institute for the Study of Human Issues